A Novice's Guide

DI...
CHURCH CHOIR

Kenneth T. Kosche

CONCORDIA PUBLISHING HOUSE · SAINT LOUIS

ISBN 0-7586-0720-2

Copyright © 2003 Concordia Publishing House
3558 S. Jefferson Avenue
St. Louis, MO 63118-3968

Manufactured in the United States of America

1 2 3 4 5 6 7 8 9 10   13 12 11 10 09 08 07 06 05 04 03

Acknowledgements

Writing a book requires a significant amount of time for the author to focus thoughts and distill into words the concepts, principles, and practices that have developed over the decades of professional and practical experience. I am grateful to Concordia University Wisconsin for granting a sabbatical, enabling me to write this resource as well as complete several music compositions.

I am indebted to Gail Black, David, and Judith Berger for their invaluable advice in shaping the musical and grammatical content of this book. Thanks is also extended to Abraham Batten for insightful suggestions about content and for illustrating conducting gestures and patterns.

God has blessed me with a loving family. Rosemary, my wife, has been especially patient and supportive in allowing me countless hours to bring this project to completion. I give to her my love and appreciation.

Finally and foremost, I give thanks to God for all the choristers on whom I have practiced my art and honed my skills for more than thirty years. They have been my teachers, responding and shaping musical thoughts, laughing at humorous anecdotes, forgiving my mistakes, and endeavoring to persistently serve Christ and His Church. I dedicate this resource to them, who have so lovingly given of themselves.

Table of Contents

Preface

- They've asked me to direct the choir but I don't really know what I'm doing.

- I'm the new pastor here and I'd like to help the choir. Nothing musical is happening right now. How can we get something going?

- They heard I played clarinet and figured I knew something about music, so I should lead the choir. Can you help me?

- My husband took a call as pastor to this congregation, and now I'm expected to lead the choir. I've only *sung* in choirs and now I'm the *director.*

Over the years I have received a number of comments and questions like the above, especially from former students, often with a sense of great urgency.

Although I offered advice each time as best I could, often I felt as though my assistance wasn't as effective as it could have been. My own library is filled with specialized books on conducting, worship, music theory, music history, dictionaries, and the like, nothing very simple or practical to loan. There is no lack of detailed, scholarly information. I have not found to my satisfaction a simple, single resource that covers the wide spectrum of issues facing a novice church choir director, a book specifically addressed to the needs of a person thrust into a situation for which he or she feels largely unprepared.

This *Novice's Guide to Conducting the Church Choir* is my response to the lack of such a resource. I make no pretenses that this book addresses comprehensively all the issues facing a church choir director. Indeed, one of the more difficult tasks for me in writing this book has been to determine what to include and what to leave out. Depending on your background, you may feel I have treated some issues in too much detail and others with not enough. At any event, I am hopeful that you will eventually want to seek out more information about all of the issues. To help start you on this life-long quest, I have included selected resources at the conclusion of the book. New materials are constantly forthcoming, although there are some trusted and valuable resources that have been available for a number of years. (Don't ignore advice merely because it was given prior to the twenty-first century.) The recommended resources I have listed should not limit you in your search for more materials, but it is a good place to begin.

There is no quick way for a beginner to gain experience. Sometimes it is helpful to glean insight from one who has "been there and done that." I hope to share with you some practical perspectives I have developed over the course of more than thirty years as a director of church choirs, school choirs, and community choruses. I've had my share of successes and failures just like any other director, and have tried to learn from both. Consequently, this guide includes material that I feel would be helpful to a beginner based upon ideas that have succeeded for me. For this reason, I recount some anecdotes here and there to flesh out particular points. Nothing in this guide is "theoretical" in the sense that I haven't tried it myself. Obviously, some things will work better for me than they might for you; I don't pretend to have all the definitive answers. For that matter, I may not even know all the *questions* yet, for you see, I am still learning. A director must never stop learning.

One of the quickest ways *to learn* a profession is to get out there and *do it*. But before you rush headlong into the choir year, please consider the advice I give you in this guide. Read it from front to back in the sequence in which I wrote it, rather than skipping around in it. Once you have done so, you can more easily refer to a part of one chapter or another as the need arises.

A common mistake novice directors make is to run out and buy copies of anthems they have recently sung with their college choirs. This may work with some church choirs, but often it does not. The simple reason for it is that church choirs bear little kinship to college choirs except for the fact that some very nice people eager to sing belong to both. After that, the similarities often end.

For this reason, we will consider people issues first and music issues later. A few years ago I had a student who said, "I want a job where I don't have to work with people." All of us have had frustrating days when we felt that way, but if such an attitude characterizes you generally, you and your choir are headed for a rocky relationship at best. God willing, this is not true for you, or you wouldn't be concerned with the issues addressed by this book in the first place.

Let's begin, then. You will become a veteran in almost no time, guaranteed. I hope this guide points you to a good beginning in a noble endeavor. God's blessings to you and your singers along the way.

Chapter 1
Understanding Singers as People

As church choir directors, we work with *people*, and our *vehicle* is music. We should focus on the people in the choir first before we concern ourselves with making music. Understanding why singers have joined the choir is vital to working with them effectively. So then, what motivates people to join church choirs? Can we generalize about some of the more important needs and expectations singers bring to the choir so that we may better understand how to relate to them? I think so, although a director might consider doing something so novel as to ask the choristers why they are eager to be part of the church choir. Then they can state their personal reasons directly. Sometimes an approach of this nature intimidates a chorister. It may even imply that a director has reservations as to whether he or she should in fact be a part of the choir. Generally, however, if one approaches the issue warmly, openly, and sincerely, the singers will respond in kind and share some valuable insights.

Joining the Choir

Broadly speaking, we can identify four significant motivations for people to join choirs, the degree for each varying from individual to individual. I believe the most important reasons people join a church choir are to sing, to minister, to learn, and to belong. There is no special reason to rank the importance of these items. They are all important, and most, if not all, of your choir members will readily acknowledge them to be their own. Where members readily embrace these, the entire choir is the beneficiary. Where members have reservations, you may be able to encourage growth in a particular area.

The most obvious motivation for joining a choir is a love for singing—this is a very significant reason. Choristers not only enjoy singing, but they enjoy singing *with others* as well. Many people believe they sound better singing in a group than alone. For them there is every reason to believe that their singing in the choir will be pleasurable. As long as singing in the choir remains a pleasure, they will keep coming to rehearsals and performances. Rarely will you find someone in a choir who does not enjoy singing, and if you do, be sure to ascertain the problem or hidden agenda, a certain signal of trouble ahead. I have only seriously encountered this issue with one particular elementary school choir in which children were forced to participate against their wishes. At the adult level, one occasionally encounters a reluctant spouse who comes to rehearsals for reasons other than a personal love for singing. Rather than despair, let this excite the "missionary" spirit in you. If you radiate a genuine love for singing yourself, your infectious enthusiasm can do wonders to win over a reluctant spirit. Generally it is "a no-brainer" that people join choirs for the love of singing.

Church choirs have an added privilege and dimension in their service—the opportunity that occurs by ministering to others though song. Beyond the joy of simply making music, they are proclaiming the very Word of the Lord. This is precisely why they come week after week, year after year, before dawn on Easter and at midnight on Christmas Eve, making tremendous sacrifices of time, often treasured *family* time. Melody and texts powerfully convey the Gospel of Jesus Christ, and choirs ardently seek to be part of this. If a servant attitude is missing in certain individuals, or worse yet, in the entire choir, you have significant work ahead of you, negotiating and readjusting attitudes. Choir members need servant-hearts invested in ministry. We'll speak more of this later.

People join church choirs to learn more about music. I have yet to find a singer whose curiosity about some aspect of music, however trivial, could not be piqued in some way. Certainly there are those whose expectations for learning can be summed up as getting all the pitches and rhythms correct in their part for every anthem—just "learning the notes." This is a noble though somewhat narrow goal. You can engage your singers to learn more about music beyond part- or note-accuracy. An early word of caution: beware of turning rehearsals into music theory or music history classes, though you can approach these topics in little doses from time to time where appropriate.

Finally, people join church choirs to belong to a group of likeminded people. After all, is this not a hallmark of the Church in which we confess to believe in "the communion of saints?" One of the blessed qualities of people who join choirs is that of loyalty, loyalty to the church, to the choir, to the director. In our modern individualistic age, loyalty to the group and its purposes is to be highly valued. Do all you can to support and sustain this worthy attitude. In my experience, choirs provide a comfortable home for "joiners." Choirs meet human social needs admirably. Though some people are naturally more reticent than others or have private personalities, true "loners" have a difficult time belonging to church choirs. Later in this chapter we will discuss some things you can do to build rapport within the choir.

Working with Volunteers

Your choir members probably are all volunteers. They do not *have* to be there; they *want* to be there, whatever their personal reasons. Part of your task as director is to keep them wanting to be there. I am not talking about pandering to individuals. You can create an atmosphere for the whole choir that is warm and inviting, productive, vital, and that affirms the value of each person as a contributing member. At the same time, you must maintain the integrity of the group. I periodically say to my choirs, "None of us is as important as all of us." This also applies to you, the director (though you have to be there). It is important that you show in your demeanor that you sincerely enjoy being with the choir. This is something for you to work at if you cannot convey this attitude easily and genuinely. Reasons *you* have for missing a rehearsal or a Sunday service are no more significant than the reasons members for being absent. You and the choir must understand this is a two-way street.

Personalities

One of the Lord's genuine blessings is the diversity of personalities found in choirs. You may not always think so, but consider this. Which one person, yourself included, would you clone for your choir if you could? Yes, wouldn't it be nice if that talented tenor had a twin, as might that reliable bass. I doubt, however, that any of us could determine one particular *personality* that we would like everyone in the choir to have. That's a good thing, because people bring a variety of perspectives and outlooks, talents and abilities to enrich the choir. Part of the joy of your job is to provide as best you can an atmosphere in the choir so that they can all contribute positively to the mix. Accomplishing this goal can be a tall order.

There are as many different personalities to deal with as there are combinations of heights and weights, hair and eye colors, age and experience in any group of people. If you like meeting people, be sure to take the time and energy to get to know your choir members as individuals. It will have a positive impact on your working together.

If you are intrigued by this sort of thing, there are various personality indices you can consult to broaden your own understanding of how diverse personalities view life. About twenty years ago I gave the short form of the Myers-Briggs personality index to one of my university choirs as part of a choir retreat. We had done something similar with the entire faculty and the resident life division. Some of the faculty became intrigued by what the results might mean as we worked in each of our respective areas. For my choir, the results were fascinating and not at all as predictable as we had thought. For example, we discovered that we had a significantly higher population of "flakes" (not a technical term) in the choir than in the general population. The "evidence" suggested that we needed to be more patient in dealing with one another when we inevitably expressed divergent points of view. That result alone was probably worth administering the test. But as the saying goes, "I *knew* that." Perhaps your curiosity will take you more deeply into this subject at your convenience.

Right now I'm not planning to be very scientific about my observations. These exaggerated and somewhat fanciful stereotypes come from many years of directing experience. You will surely encounter one or a mix of the following choir personality traits in the seemingly most heterogeneous groups:

Extroverts: They beam at you with confidence when they sing, sometimes almost forcing you to look away from them. They interrupt your rehearsal to ask you to play the tenor part on the top of page 3. They stand up to sing before you signal them to do so. They start passing back music when the choir has finished singing it. If you were not officially in charge of the choir, you know who would be (and every now and then you wonder who *really* runs the organization).

Introverts: They may have a hard time looking at you when you are directing, especially if you look their way often. If you want them to sing their parts alone, they demur, or ask to sing with others. They privately confide to you that they prefer to sing *second* soprano. They dutifully put the piles of passed-in music in order.

Managers: They keep track of robes and choir folders. They worry that the choir will never learn all the music you have selected in time for Christmas. They keep mental tabs on tardiness and absence. They have incredible memories of past choir exploits. They worry about the budget. They watch the clock.

Entrepreneurs: They bring you programs from other choirs. They buy music for the choir that they think you should sing (occasionally asking you first). They serve as the choir's early warning system and blunt criticism of the director or the choir out in the narthex before you are even aware of it. They unlock the doors and turn the lights on in the choir room before you arrive. Sometimes they irritate you by their *over-commitment* to the choir. They can be fiercely loyal and supportive. (If you can, make sure at least one of these is elected to the Board of Elders or Trustees/Property Management.)

Well, I told you this wouldn't be very scientific! But trust me. These portraits *are* realistic. You will encounter a very wide variety of personality types in your choir. First, thank God for the fact. Engage the different personalities, insights, and perspectives to the advantage of the whole choir. Permit each person to make a particular contribution to the working together of the group — musically, spiritually, administratively, socially, educationally, and financially. Try to get as many people as you can involved in some aspect of the choir's work, however seemingly insignificant. There are more potential contributors to your choir than you might first imagine. They just do it in different ways with different styles.

Leadership within the choir takes many forms. Some leaders work more quietly and others more overtly. The so-called "difficult personality" is often an overt type holding genuine and deeply felt concerns about aspects of the choir that he or she feels are being neglected. In some cases, you can publicly thank the individual for being so perceptive as to identify these concerns. In other cases, it may be appropriate to reassure the individual that you have matters well in hand. The late Dr. Walter Stuenkel used to comment that in every congregation there are what he termed "alligators." ("Alligator" is so much more *graphic* than "difficult personality!") You know what he meant, people who range about, always snapping at things. Sometimes you are afraid to get too close to them lest they take a bite out of you. His solution? "Drain the swamp!" I take him to mean that if you remove the reason for the person to be snappish, the person no longer can legitimately act like an "alligator." Usually this works, though there are those unfortunate souls who, despite everyone's best efforts, still go about baring "alligator" teeth. Pray for them and stay out of their reach.

Rapport

Rapport is such a positive term! It is one of those relational terms that most easily defines itself by its presence or absence. How well you get along with your choir and they with you is a measure of your rapport. There is no such thing as "instant rapport." It must be built over time. Some directors have an easier time than others establishing rapport with their choir. There are no sure-fire, magic solutions that will work for everyone to establish rapport, though there are some things I can tell you to avoid. Generally, common sense will inform you when you are on the right track or not. For example, pleasant people usually elicit pleasant responses and critical people elicit critical responses. It's almost a corollary to one of the laws of physics: for every action there is an equal and opposite reaction. Can you be pleasant when faced with a differing opinion? Can you critique the choir without being hypercritical? As director you will discover soon enough that to a great extent the choir will mirror your most overt personality traits (what a scary thought!) This is both a blessing and a curse. If you encounter relational difficulties with your choir, it may be helpful to examine first the attitudes you project to the choir before you become critical of them.

One personal trait that can create or destroy rapport very quickly relates to how you wear the mantle of authority. People who have a high degree of self-assurance generally do not need to assert their authority vigorously. If you are in command of yourself, you can be in charge of other people more easily than if you feel insecure. If your insecurities stem from a personal lack of skill or self-confidence in musical matters, you have to practice and develop your skills to gain the requisite self-confidence. It is no good pretending to know something if you do not, especially if there are choir members who know more than you do. Which is worse, a person with great musical skills and little self-confidence, or a person of decidedly modest gifts and over-confidence? Just guessing, I'd say the second person may get more accomplished, but I'm not sure a brash approach establishes effective rapport with others.

It is important to remember that your authority as director naturally covers musical and spiritual matters that relate to the choir. In these areas you should not make decisions by majority vote. A little gimmick I use when necessary is to suggest that we do things democratically—*my* way! ("Everyone who votes for an E-flat here, please raise your hand...") However, when it comes to matters like wearing robes or not in the

14

church's balcony on a hot day or scheduling people to bring treats for the after-choir coffee klatch, you may actually score points with the choir by delegating the decision to them or to an individual in the choir. In other words, assert yourself in matters where you are naturally in charge and avoid needless controversy in areas of indifference. Wisdom lies in knowing when to do which.

Refer for a moment to the four motivations listed previously for joining church choirs. The more you and the choir members are in accord about these matters, the more easily you build rapport. If there are areas of disagreement about the choir's purpose and goals, rapport is harmed. Let's return for a moment to the second motivation, joining the choir to minister. Concert choirs and church choirs differ greatly in this respect. If your background has been heavily influenced by your participation in a choir oriented to giving concerts, you need to pay special attention to this factor. Let me illustrate this point.

Over the years I have been blessed to work with several church choirs having genuine servants' hearts. They knew and understood ministry. I recall one occasion with a particular choir when I leaned across the piano at the beginning of a rehearsal and said, "You know, we have about *four hundred years experience together* in this choir!" Well, of course, there were some startled facial expressions at first, but they quickly understood what I meant. Forty faithful people had spent one rehearsal night each week for ten months of the year, forty-five or more Sundays per year, including many summer Sunday mornings (both services), Advent and Lenten Wednesdays, Thanksgiving, Christmas season and Holy Week, three services on Easter morning, and even a number of funerals, engaging *together* in *musical ministry.* You guessed it. This was my tenth anniversary as director of that choir. Just think of it: four hundred years of musical *ministry together!*

You need to encourage such servant attitudes whenever you can. Simultaneously, you need to continue to encourage fine musicianship for the sake of *effective* ministry, not for enhancing the stature of the choir, for aesthetic reasons, for educational purposes, or for anything that takes precedence over ministry or draws attention to itself and away from the proclamation of the Gospel. On the contrary, work hard to adorn the Gospel with the finest quality singing of which your choir is capable. This is the choir's noblest ministry. Working together toward the goal of effective ministry accomplished through excellent singing will build rapport like nothing else I can think of. The motivation is intrinsic. It is not something imposed by you or by someone else from outside the scope of the church choir's natural mission and purpose.

Commitment

The anecdote above illustrates a positive attitude by a group toward ministry, a great commitment on the part of all the individuals in the group. Commitment is another term defined more clearly by its presence or absence, though sometimes we mistake the signs. For the success of any group endeavor, commitment to the group by all the members is essential. This is not a novel idea. We use this term freely about athletic teams. Coaches preach it. Sports writers decry its absence. The term applies in equal measure to the church choir. I define commitment to the church choir as the willingness of each member to attend rehearsals regularly, to learn and sing the music to the best of his or her ability, and to show up for any and all performances on time, prepared to sing. Sporadic attendance, frequent tardiness, and lack-luster singing appear to demonstrate lack of commitment. Sometimes, however, what may seem to be a lack of commitment in reality is the inability of a choir member to make a *long-term* commitment.

Unfortunately, many people find it more difficult to make long-term commitments to the church choir now than in years past. We find some underlying reasons for this in society in general. For most people, the church no longer defines the center of their social universe. For others, the changing employment scene forces choices upon them they would prefer not to have to make. For yet others, family or personal circumstances entice them to periodic absences. America is a very mobile society. A recent statistic I heard indicates that only about half of Americans currently live within fifty miles of their birthplaces; another relates that, on the average, Americans change residence seven times in their lives. As the face of America changes, so does the face of your church choir. This fact poses some unique though not insurmountable challenges.

Setting aside the occasional member's illness, it is no longer generally realistic to expect all the members of your choir to be present at all rehearsals and performances week in and week out for nine or ten months of the year. Fifteen years ago, if I occasionally asked for the choir to sing in *both* services on Sunday, there was hardly a dissenting voice. This is no longer true. Mid-week rehearsals fare similarly. Fifteen years ago a

16

member would be conspicuously absent. Now some members are seasonal "snow birds." Others are away traveling for several weeks at a time. New members are cautious about joining the choir because they do not wish to be "tied down." High schoolers may come for a week or two, but then the activities at school or at their part-time jobs command their attention. If you are an impatient person, choir directing may not be for you. Phrased more positively, working with the volunteer church choir is the Lord's special way to teach you patience and flexibility.

You may have to accept short-term commitments or seasonal participation by some members. You may need to schedule rehearsals more flexibly. It is possible to find a sense of excitement and joy in creating a family choir in which parents and their children can unite their voices in song, though this may mean selecting or arranging special repertoire to accommodate the situation. A key to success in addition to patience and flexibility is *creativity*.

Over the years I have adopted an attitude which places me less in the role of "Solomon" to judge valid and less valid reasons for absence, a role, by the way, that I am not wise enough or pretentious enough to play. I simply view an absence as an absence, tardiness as tardiness. When you think about it, the *reason* does not change the *result*. Objectively viewed, a singer is simply absent or late. You ultimately have little control over the situation; you *do* have control over *how you react* to it. If you genuinely believe a choir member's absence or tardiness is hurting the choir, it is your duty to tell the member *privately* and *in a timely fashion*. It may be that there is something you need to know about the member that is not a public matter. Perhaps the absence or tardiness didn't actually harm the work of the choir. Part of your responsibility to the choir is dispassionately assessing the point. You and the member mutually need to address the issue without your placing a value judgment on the *reasons* for the behavior. In my first teaching position, a wise and experienced junior high principal told me, "Always leave a parent a back door for his child's behavior. You may be dead right, but the parent will hate you for it." There is a corollary here for the church choir. I think a choir director is safer in dealing with the *consequences to the choir* of an absence than in judging the *validity* of it. Both parties may view the consequences more objectively without necessarily destroying interpersonal relationships in the process. Maybe the member can act to correct the problem, which benefits everyone. Yes, leaders are called upon to make difficult decisions at times.

Perhaps you could say much of the discussion so far has been common sense. I hope that it is, both *common* and *sensible*. It amazes me, however, that many church choir directors, young and not so young, place an overwhelming importance on music making rather than on the people who make the music. If ministry is the goal, people are the ministers, music the vehicle. I think it is important to keep this principle in proper perspective for yourself and your choir.

Chapter 2
Understanding People as Singers

It is time now to turn our attention to musical matters. Although this book focuses significantly on adult choirs, I believe the principles enunciated so far apply to children as well. There is a danger, however, in treating children like miniature adults. This is true on a number of levels.

Intellectually: Young children cannot think as abstractly as adults.
Emotionally: Experience broadens and deepens the range of a person's emotions.
Spiritually: Though children often put adults to shame in matters of implicit faith, they may be limited in their responses because of their inexperience in life.
Physically: Children do not possess the vocal range or the lung capacity of adults.

Problems arise when directors select music for children written specifically for adults, when publishers fail to provide music written for children, or when they convey the impression that all their publications for treble voices, unison, or two-part choirs, can be sung as appropriately by children as by adults. Be thoughtful when selecting children's choral literature, being especially careful to consider the characteristics of children's voices.

Characteristics of Children's Voices

Young children *love* to sing. It is important that you give them music appropriate to their intellectual, emotional, spiritual, and physical needs. Specifically, the music must conform to their proper vocal ranges, and they must use a true *singing* voice. The old saw about using "inside voices" and "outside voices" may have implications for decorum, but it does not translate to proper singing technique. One or two children shouting on the playground can be louder than a small choir of children singing, but no one should rightly confuse a shouting voice with a singing voice. I once reminded a well-intentioned lady who was encouraging her young Sunday school charges to make more sound using their playground voices, "If you want more sound, please get more kids!"

Consult in particular the gold mine of materials prepared by Helen Kemp regarding children's voices and vocal production.

Generally speaking, until the onset of voice change in adolescence, the following practical ranges represent what most children should be able to sing as primary and middle grade school-aged children.

Figure 1
Children's Voice Ranges

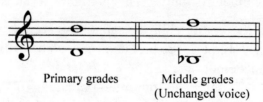

Primary grades   Middle grades
                        (Unchanged voice)

Let's define three important terms before we go further. One is *range*, another is *tessitura*, and a third is *timbre*. Simply put, *range* refers to the pitches a person can sing from the lowest to the highest. *Tessitura* can be defined as the "comfort zone" within the total range. *Timbre* describes the tone quality of a voice, not in the sense of being pleasant or unpleasant, but the quality that makes you sound like you and me sound like me, even though we are singing the same pitch.

A singer may have a wide range, that is, may be able to reach quite high and quite low sounds, but the person's voice will wear out if he or she is asked to sing high or sing low over an extended period of time. Think of tessitura as an "inner range" of the most comfortable half dozen or so consecutive pitches for a person to sing, usually around the middle of the range. Most of the pitches in a singer's music should match the singer's tessitura. Singing at the extremes of one's range, high or low, results in vocal strain and a tired or damaged voice over the long-term. Also, you can hear a marked change in vocal timbre, sometimes abruptly from one pitch to another, when a singer pushes the voice strongly from the bottom of the range to the top. You have heard joking references to "belting out" a few bars of music, I'm sure. "Belting" is actually a term to describe pushing the voice with a heavy sound into too high a range. This practice stems from Broadway musicals. ("There's *no* business like *show* business...") Think of driving your car at 40 mph in first gear, and you have a comparable metaphor. Children especially should not belt or force a heavy sound high in their vocal range, nor should they sing near

20

the bottom of their range for a long time, something popular music frequently demands.

By all means, encourage children to sing in parts. When singing in parts, it is wise to have some children sing the "first part" in one piece and switch to the "second part" in another. This practice develops their ranges and musicianship. Children occasionally mistakenly believe they are "sopranos for life" because they always sing the top melody part. Others believe themselves to be "altos" for the same reason regarding harmony parts. In truth, these terms describing adult range categories are inappropriate for most children until at least high school age, and in some cases, until college. Furthermore, most women and men develop into "middle voices" called *mezzo-sopranos* and *baritones* as adults. "Mezzo" means "middle." Use simple and neutral terms such as "part one" and "part two" to avoid the problems of inappropriate early voice categorization.

Before their voices change, boys and girls possess approximately the same vocal range. In fact, boys often sing with a rounder and fuller *timbre*. In a blind test, boys' singing voices are virtually indistinguishable from girls' to the average listener. During adolescence, voice ranges and timbres begin to change seemingly overnight. In reality, voice change is a longer, slower process. The "overnight" observation may be due to the fact that voices change at different rates beginning at different times. The early teen-age years can become a confusing time for singers and directors alike. It may surprise you to know that girls also undergo voice change, though theirs is not nearly so dramatic a change. A technical term used for voice change is voice *mutation*. Historically, opinions about voice mutation have differed radically. Solid scientific research in recent years supports conclusions reported by John Cooksey, Anthony Barresi, and others. Detailed descriptions of male and female voice mutation at this point counters the purpose of a "novice's guide." My dilemma at this point arises from trying to give you a simplified summary of complex information in a way that is also accurate. Since even "the experts" have disagreed, I cannot convey all the information for you in only a few pages. You have further reading to do for homework. *Figure 2* is an excerpt from *Working with Adolescent Voices* by Dr. Cooksey. I strongly recommend that you read "Section 1: Establishing a Foundation" for a more detailed presentation about boys' and girls' voice changes.

In *Figure 2* below, ranges are the distances between the white notes and recommended tessituras the distance between the black notes. Please understand that the term "New Baritone" according to Cooksey's definition does not directly correspond to the term "baritone" in adult voice classification. You can expect the voice change process to begin for many boys in the sixth grade.

Figure 2

Mean Ranges and Tessituras for the Male Voice Change Stages

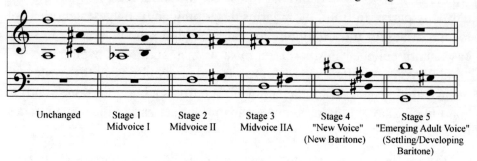

Unchanged	Stage 1	Stage 2	Stage 3	Stage 4	Stage 5
	Midvoice I	Midvoice II	Midvoice IIA	"New Voice" (New Baritone)	"Emerging Adult Voice" (Settling/Developing Baritone)

Girls usually begin their process of voice change earlier than boys, some as early as age 11. The severity of the change for girls regarding range is much less. Remember, boys' voices will be dropping at least an octave in pitch before they are finished. You will often notice the onset of voice change first in the speaking voices of boys and girls. You will notice boys speaking at a lower pitch or having a pitch control problem. Girls tend to exhibit huskiness and/or breathiness when their voices start to change. Some have a very "thin" timbre. Too often directors label the huskier voices "alto" and the lighter, thinner voices "soprano." Doing so at this time is a huge mistake, since these vocal manifestations are not necessarily true to the ultimate range and timbre of their later adult voices. As I mentioned above, it is healthy and wise to have girls alternate between so-called soprano and alto parts to develop their musicianship (the voice parts function differently musically) and vocal range. True soprano and alto voices comprise a smaller segment of the total female population than do mezzo-sopranos. Consequently it is better for their sakes not to rush to hasty judgments. Let them remain "middle voices" until they confirm their true vocal colors, perhaps by the time they are of college age or into their early twenties. If a young lady genuinely experiences a tired or strained voice singing in a certain range over time, consider moving her to a part that is higher or lower temporarily. Other factors such as her vocal production need to be considered in making this decision. For example, she may be singing improperly. Alternating between soprano and alto parts in modestly ranged music will allow her to settle into her proper vocal role when the time is right for her.

In practical terms, you can expect most girls to sing comfortably in the range given above in *Figure 1* for unchanged voices until they demonstrate that they can sing several pitches higher with ease. Others seem to exhibit more strength toward the bottom of their range. Once again using the automobile analogy, beware allowing a young woman to sing 40 mph in low gear at the bottom of her range. This is a faithful saying: *there are no natural female tenors.* Young or older adult women who sing in "tenor" range sing dysfunctionally, risking permanent injury to their voices.

Practically, you may experience differences between what boys and girls actually sound like and what they theoretically should be singing given appropriate coaching. Be prepared to do several things:

1. Test each voice individually to determine each voice range.
2. Be prepared for occasional surprise changes in the boys' ranges.
3. Give singers music in the same ranges as their voices. Adult tenor and bass music probably is inappropriately pitched for most of the boys, as are low alto parts for the girls.
4. Seriously inform yourself and your singers further about this topic.

Since you are perceptive, you will have guessed by now that it is difficult to find a satisfactory range for adolescent boys to sing in unison. Unison singing by a mixed voice group is even more difficult. The range of many unison songs will be too high for some singers and too low for others, a situation you can solve by singing in parts. But that raises other issues. When we speak of unison singing by mixed voices, we assume the lower octave of the same pitches as being in "unison." Cooksey suggests a composite range for unison singing by changing and unchanged voices, shown in *Figure 3*. You can see that tunes in the keys of B-flat and C stand the greatest chance for successful unison singing by this age group.

Figure 3
Composite Unison Range
for Unchanged and Changing Voices

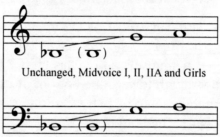

Unchanged, Midvoice I, II, IIA and Girls

A final word before we move on. Adolescents who say they dislike singing have often succumbed to peer pressure, become jaded because of what they are given to sing in music classes in school, or as is unfortunately true in the case of many boys, decide that singing isn't "macho." Voice mutation for girls does not cause them the degree of distress that it does for boys. Many boys drop out of choirs because they cannot deal effectively with their changing voices. This was certainly the case for me. As a seventh grader, I sang the lead second soprano in our parish school choir with a strong, clear voice. I learned music easily and I loved to sing. Then my voice changed, and neither the director nor I knew what to do about it. Subsequently, I quit the choir, not to sing in a school choir again until my senior year in high school. Forty years later you are reading my book. Thank the Lord, not all bad experiences are fatal. One can only wonder how many young male singers we lose when their voices change, fending for themselves vocally. Talk to your boys and explain as best you can what is happening to them. You can at least demystify one of life's early crises for them, and they *will* listen to you. Try it, and see for yourself.

Characteristics of Adult Voices

We need to make a distinction between *emerging* adult voices and *mature* adult voices regarding range, tessitura, and timbre. Quite a few young voices are still in the process of voice change well into and beyond high school. Boys, who mature physically later than girls, continue to exhibit the voice ranges described in *Figure 2* in high school. These factors contribute to the timbre of the various choirs. The average listener has no difficulty in distinguishing the sounds of a high school choir, a college choir, or an adult choir of the "forty and above crowd" (the population of many of our church choirs).

Figure 4, based on my experience, shows you my ideas of practical, conservative SATB ranges for more mature adult church choir singers in white notes and the still settling high school (including some college-aged) singers in black notes. I don't mean for you to infer that you cannot exceed these ranges. However, staying within these ranges 90% or more of the time will assure positive results for your singers in tone production and vocal health. It is not safe to assume your singers automatically conform to these ranges. Have them sing for you privately and without any fanfare to discover exactly what ranges they can sing. Pick a well-known hymn tune like "Beautiful Savior" ("Fairest Lord Jesus"), which has a range of an octave, that you can also start a little higher and lower, or have them sing some scales on "Ah" or "Oh." Better yet, have them sing the hymn on "Ah" or "Oh" (which works well for people who haven't memorized more than the first line of words to the hymn). It's more fun singing a tune than singing scales.

Figure 4
Practical Ranges for Mature and Still Settling Adult Voices

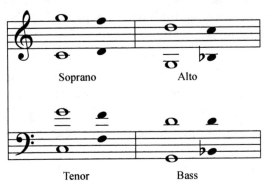

It is a mistake to select music that forces young singers to exert their voices toward extremes of range, either high or low. With rare exception, neither new altos nor new basses sing with any *gravitas*, nor can most produce certain low tones. Therefore, it is unwise to expect it of them. Mature choristers, especially with a little vocal training, can easily negotiate a range of an octave and a fifth or slightly more. Younger and untrained voices find this more difficult. A practical case in point: the American national anthem has a range of an octave and a fifth. The next time you are at the ballpark, pay attention to the singing around you. How many people can either sing the entire tune or sound equally pleasant throughout the song's range? "Oh-oh, *saaaay...*" "O'er the land of the *freeeee...*" (By the way, how well do *you* fare with the Anthem?)

Remember, I told you earlier that most adult voices are middle voices: mezzo-soprano or baritone. Unfortunately, due to the general lack of tenors, too many young baritones either eagerly volunteer or are conscripted to sing tenor. I hold to an untested theory that we do not generally develop tenors properly when boys' voices change. Indeed, many young men relish the new deep, buzzy sounds of their emerging adult voices and only reluctantly sing in a lighter "head voice," though it is exactly the technique they need to negotiate the higher pitches. Because a young man can sing in a light, high range is no guarantee by itself that he is a tenor rather than a lyric baritone. You need to factor range and timbre together. Concerning *timbre*, tenors generally sing with brightness rather than fullness throughout their range. Concerning *range*, tenors make little or *no* sound singing downward as they near B-flat (*Figure 4*). If you audition a potential tenor only to discover that he can sing below B-flat, he is probably a baritone, although he may have a high range as well.

By the way, tenor parts are written variously in the clefs shown below in *Figure 5*. You need only familiarize yourself with the first three, the most common. Example 1 is the clef bass voices use (hence the term "bass clef") and is usually the clef for combining tenor and bass parts on one staff. The little "8" which hangs down on the bottom of the next clef indicates that the pitches sound an octave lower than they would if treble voices were singing (hence the term "treble clef"). Example 3 is used interchangeably with example 2, and it is the real treble clef. One assumes that if men are singing the part, they will sound in their proper octave. Example 4 is the moveable "C" clef called "tenor clef" because it is specifically designed for tenors. You will find this clef printed in music from the seventeenth and eighteenth centuries (Bach, for instance), though modern scores usually translate this clef to one of the first two. In this case, "middle C" is the second line down from the top, the idea being to keep most of the pitches a tenor would sing on the staff itself without adding leger lines. I have listed examples 5 and 6 only because you may run across these very odd looking clefs and wonder what in the world they mean. Musically, pitches for examples 5 and 6 read like example 2.

Figure 5
Clefs Used for Tenor Parts

What is true for men is somewhat the reverse for women. You are more likely to have fewer genuine altos than sopranos. Many of your "altos" are really mezzo-sopranos, or they are sopranos singing low. Sometimes this has resulted from early voice typing, because as adolescents they sang with a fuller sound and also excelled at sight-reading. As the unfortunate saying goes, "Any dummy can sing the melody, but an alto has to sight-read." Before you dismiss this chauvinistic sentiment, let me emphasize that I have experienced the effects of this thinking repeatedly over the years, especially when auditioning women for a community-based choir. Some would-be-altos feigned near heart failure when I demonstrated quite clearly to them that they had mistakenly sung in the alto range for over twenty years, although physiologically they were sopranos, some lyric and high sopranos at that. Once again, consider both range and timbre in the decision. A true alto sings with warmth and fullness in the bottom two-thirds of her range, not simply in "chest voice" for five or six bottom notes, being unable to transition smoothly up over an F. Use the same test for women as for men described above, having them sing down to B-flat below middle C. Altos are able to sing with the same timbre to about G, whereas sopranos have little or no strength in this range, although they may be able to sing as low as G. Even though they can do so, it is still best not to have the altos sing below B-flat too frequently.

For some reason, much music is written that locks the alto part into a small range around D, E, and F. Typically, soprano parts soar with the melody. Bass parts range around with interesting leaps because they set the chord functions. Tenors complement the movement of the sopranos in tenor range. Altos are pluggers. They fill in the missing notes, often with very uninteresting little parts. Unfortunately, some altos get so used to this that they make a career out of these three notes. Some altos develop an especially edgy sound in this range, born of too frequent practice. Did you ever sit in front of an alto singing *her* part of "Beautiful

27

Savior"? She can virtually cut through steel in her alto fervor, and she invariably has the part memorized! Consequently, when I play the organ for this hymn, I change the harmony just to confound her (and make her think of singing the lovely, wide-ranging tune). Flexible singing is important. Try to pick music that exercises as much of your singers' natural ranges as possible to develop a free singing tone.

Common Choral Combinations

A choir can be comprised of many different combinations of voices. Most music you purchase has been written or arranged for the more usual assortments of treble voices, men's voices, or some combination of mixed voices usually labeled "SATB" or "SAB." This is not to say there are no other combinations published, but these are the most logical combinations to start with.

Treble Choirs

Treble choirs can be comprised of children with unchanged voices, women, or a combination of the two. You will find music written for unison voices through four parts, though the bulk of treble choir music seems to be for two and three parts. In two-part writing, the composer sometimes writes the music "for equal voices," which is to say, you may distribute your singers easily between the parts because both parts will have nearly the same range. This sort of music is ideal for the practice I suggested earlier: moving singers from part one in a piece to part two in another. If the parts are labeled "SA" (soprano and alto), check the respective ranges of each part. Swapping parts with groups of singers may still be possible if the composite ranges and tessituras are not very different. Otherwise, you will need to assign singers appropriately to higher or lower parts. Three-part writing usually implies at least one lower part, though you can find occasional three-part music scored for equal voices. Usually this is called "SSA" rather than "SAA." The second "S" is a mezzo-soprano part, unless the soprano parts are of equal range. You can scan through a piece to verify the ranges, your eye quickly taking in more or less the top and bottom pitches of a part as you glance through it. Some composers write "SSAA" four-part treble music, but unless the parts overlap from time to time, beware that the second alto part may be written too low or may simply stay in the lowest range. Enjoyable alto parts are melodic rather than harmonic. Effectively written alto parts *don't* have the same musical characteristics as bass parts only in a higher octave. This is one reason it is possible to write pleasing two- and three-part treble music, especially if there is some sort of accompaniment to provide a harmonic basis.

Male Choirs

It may strike you as odd that though more treble voices are usually available to you than male voices, treble music is typically written in two or three parts while male chorus music is typically written in four parts, "TTBB." The reason for frequent four-part writing is the way the voices function in men's music. Here one usually finds a true bass part. The other voices supply harmonic and melodic components as needed, and it often takes four parts to make the composition work effectively. Even so, in much of men's music, the middle two parts or the top two parts will cross one another frequently or be identical now and again, so that there are four parts only when a full chord is needed. Unison men's singing can sound strong and effective, as can "TB" two-part singing. Occasionally you can borrow "SA" music and have the men sing it in their respective ranges. You may have noted in *Figure 4* that I suggest that sopranos and tenors sing approximately the same ranges although an octave apart, as do altos and basses. While generally true, you will find mature basses who can sing a third or fourth below this range. I have already cautioned not to use too much music with a very low alto part. If you had to adapt it for the bass, it would not explore the full extent of the bass range. For this reason, "SA" music doesn't automatically transfer to "TB," all other factors being acceptable. Three-part music can be either "TTB" or "TBB." Check to see if your baritones can comfortably sing the middle part whether it is labeled "T" or "B." Four-part "TTBB" music often contains a fairly high tenor part to prevent the voices from being all muddled together. Your tenors will rise to the challenge of an occasional high note (pardon the pun). Truth be known, they will *glory* in it. However, first examine the music for its tessitura as well as its range. Conquering a high note gives tenors satisfaction. Living in thin air kills them.

Mixed Choirs

The standard configuration for mixed voices is "SATB." Of course, you must immediately determine whether your choir has a good balance of singers for all parts. You may consider using "two-part mixed" compositions to your advantage. Well-written "two-part mixed" music stays comfortably in the middle of the respective voice ranges so that it can be effectively sung by mixed choirs that do not have an acceptable balance among sections. Though the occasional piece belies the rule, performing "SA" as "two-part mixed" may not musically satisfy singers or listeners. You have a better chance trying this with "TB" music because the bass part already functions like a bass, and the tenor part probably contains the melody. Of course, tenors may find singing with the bass difficult in this case because the music was written for the range and tessitura of bass in the first place. Some two-part music sounds acceptable with higher voices (soprano and tenor) singing the upper part and lower voices (alto and bass) singing the lower part. The sound is sometimes "muddy" because of all the octaves crossing over one another. You have to become sensitive to the differences to judge appropriately.

The "Tenor-less" Choir

No tenors? This problem would seemingly be easily resolved by "SAB" music. Indeed, you can find some lovely "SAB" pieces that are musically effective and suit your choir personnel admirably. Unfortunately, in my judgment, too much music written for "SAB" voices is ineffective musically and difficult to sing because of the voice ranges. Some composers write a "B" part that would tax even the best singer. The part ranges all over the place, occasionally too low for a tenor and occasionally too high for a bass. The soprano gets the melody, and the alto part, true to stereotype, gets the leftover notes, which are usually too low. It is not uncommon for "SAB" music to have an alto part rarely rising up to the staff but instead dwelling only on leger lines below the staff. Other ineffective "SAB" music merely leaves out the tenor line from an otherwise "SATB" arrangement and attempts to fill in the missing notes with the piano accompaniment. Check the Resources section for some SAB selections that you may find attractive.

Chapter 3
Getting a Good Sound

Having considered the range, tessitura, and timbre of individual voices, we now turn to the sound of the whole choir. It stands to reason that
if individuals in the choir sing well, the sound of the entire group benefits. Yet, it is as possible to have a collection of fine voices that do not
sound beautiful together as it is to have a collection of so-so voices that
give a very pleasing and musical sound. Think of "Choral Tone" as the
hub of a wheel. Radiating from the hub are factors that influence the
sound of the choir, eight of which I have placed into *Figure 6* below.
Each of these inter-related factors influences the sound of the choir in
some way.

Figure 6
Influences on Choral Tone

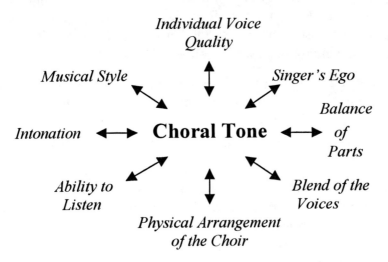

It would work to our advantage to determine a plan of action to
enhance the choral tone by dealing with several of these factors all at one
time. Which of the eight factors above do you think most generally helps
the singers better to hear the sound of the whole choir, to blend their
voices, to balance the sections, and to sing in tune (four of the factors in
Figure 6)?

Seating the Choir

I believe that factor is the physical arrangement of the choir, or as I have termed it, "seating the choir." *Figure 7* shows several ways to arrange a mixed voice choir.

Figure 7
Placement of Sections in the Choir

1. "Back to Front"	2. "Side-by-Side"	3. "Enclave"

MEN WOMEN	W	W O M E N
not	M O	
WOMEN MEN	E M	W M W
	N E	E
	N	W N W

Arrangement 1, "Back to Front" gets its name for obvious reasons. I prefer to place the men behind the women for the acoustic advantage this gives. Men sing the lower tones to form the harmonic basis for the choir. It is far easier to adjust intonation and balance with this formation than with the women singing behind the men.

Arrangement 2, "Side by Side" can be reversed just as easily, however. This placement is advantageous principally when singing music that divides the choir into a men's chorus and a women's chorus. Otherwise the placement advantages of arrangement 1 far outweigh those of arrangement 2.

Arrangement 3, which I have called "Enclave," is most advantageous if the women significantly outnumber the men. When the men sing from the center front they project better than from the center back or from one row spread across the back. I suppose we could fantasize about having far more men than women in our church choir, but, as my students say, "Get real!" You may also wish to resort to the "Enclave" situation if your junior choir contains either few boys with changed voices or few boys, period. In either case, you may group the boys together, but put those with unchanged or Stage I (Midvoice I) voices at the edge of the boys' section next to girls singing their same part. In that way the boys do not feel conspicuous by their presence in the girls' section, though they would otherwise be there because of their voices.

Whether the choir sings chordal (*homophonic*) or highly melodic (*polyphonic*) music, it is more effective to group singers for each voice part in the same physical location so they can hear one another better and you can direct them more easily. (I'll explain "homophonic" and "polyphonic" under "Musical Styles.") Although a mixed formation has a valid use, I do not recommend beginning directors to use it except for the occasional time in rehearsals when it is an enjoyable change of pace to have people "scramble," standing next to singers of different voice parts.

Example 1, "Back to Front" is more or less the norm for mixed choirs. I want you to consider how you will place the basses and tenors in relation to the sopranos and altos. *Figure 8* shows the four ways to do this along with my recommendations.

Figure 8
Placement of Voice Parts in the Choir

B	T		B	T
		not		
S	A		A	S

or

T	B		T	B
		not		
A	S		S	A

These placements further refine *Figure 7*, Example 1. Not only are balance and intonation assisted by placing the men behind the women, but intonation is also significantly improved by having the basses behind the sopranos and the tenors behind the altos. We call the soprano and bass "polar" voices because they represent the highest and the lowest tones of the choir. The tonality of the music depends on tuning to the bass. The inner voices, alto and tenor, provide important components to the harmony, but they do not set the tuning for the choir. In fact, even though the altos and tenors may be singing perfectly on pitch, the intonation ("in tune-ness") of the choir will suffer if either or both the sopranos and basses sing out of tune. Bass intonation is the more crucial of the two. This is not to suggest that your choir cannot sing in tune if it is physically arranged differently. When the basses stand behind the sopranos it is easier to sing in tune for fundamental acoustical reasons.

If the size or shape of your performance space constrains you, and you must place the singers side by side in only one row, then try one of the following arrangements that address as closely as possible the principles enunciated in *Figure 8*. These also work for very small choirs or quartets. Notice, in each case, the basses are next to the sopranos and the tenors next to the altos. In one case, the men are together and in the other the women are together. If you have fewer men, use either of the first two examples, and *vice versa.*

Figure 9
Side-by-Side Mixed Choir Formations

S B T A   or   **A T B S**   or   **B S A T**   or   **T A S B**

Finally, precisely where and on what basis do you decide to place each individual within the grand framework? Some choirs arrange themselves without your intervention on the basis of their friendships, tradition, height, random seating patterns, musical abilities, levels of self-confidence, or other reasons. Most of these are not intrinsically musical reasons.

Seating on the basis of friendships, one of the most common ways choristers arrange themselves, recommends itself best for providing chatting opportunities in rehearsal.

Tradition is a loaded term. When we have no intrinsic reason to defend a practice, we appeal to "tradition," as in, "We've *always* done it that way before!" Start a new tradition by focusing the choir on valid *musical* reasons for decisions.

Placement on the basis of height provides an appealing look when the group performs in front of an audience, but since most church choirs sing from the choir loft anyway, this usually is a moot point. I'm not even sure I'd do this when placing the elementary school choir on the risers for their Christmas program. So unless you're going for the "organ pipe" look, disregard height as an important factor. If your choir loves to test your memory by always sitting in different places, you or they may have some fun, but there is no worthwhile musical reason to do this. Such movement negates many of the listening skills a choir develops over time in rehearsals. For this reason alone, try to have the choir sit or stand in the same formation for both rehearsals and performances.

The final two arrangements are intrinsically more musical: placement on the basis of musical abilities, and the closely related factor, placement on the basis of the self-confidence levels of your choristers. Some directors like to place a confident singer next to a less-confident singer to encourage the weaker member. There may be times to do this, but my experience has shown me that weak singers never become strong singers when they know someone else will be there to prompt them. "Oh, we can't possibly sing this piece! So-and-so isn't here and I always follow him/her!" This short-term solution builds long-term dependency. I wouldn't rely on it as a practice unless I didn't care about my singers' musical growth and development.

I use a variation of a practice developed by Weston Noble, director of the Nordic Choir at Luther College, Decorah, Iowa. He places singers next to each other in a continuum of "intense" voices to "less intense" voices. Loosely defined, intensity denotes a combination of the "size" of each voice, its timbre, and its vibrato rate. The premise is that singers sing more naturally and freely when they are next to singers of a similar voice quality. Good intonation results more easily, and blend receives an immediate assist when neighboring voices don't "fight" with each other, or when one or several singers are forced to shape their sounds severely to bridge the vocal disparity. In this *novice's* guide, I chose not to go into greater detail at this point other than to suggest that you try a choir formation in which more intense voices are grouped toward the center of the choir (in their respective sections, of course) and progressively less intense voices radiate outward, as in *Figure 10*. Such a formation minimizes the propensity of individual voices to stand out. Though intended as a compliment, I don't receive it as such when someone says, "My goodness, your choir sounds so good! I especially like the sound of the third singer from the right in the second row." For your choir to have a good sound, voices need to blend, not stand out.

Figure 10

Placement of Individual Voices by Vocal Intensity

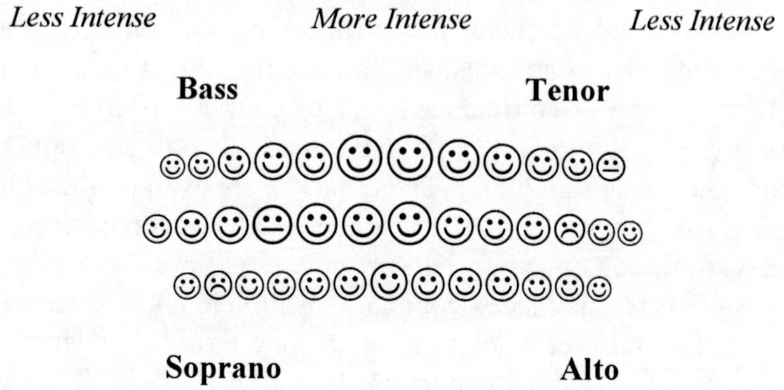

Less Intense   *More Intense*   *Less Intense*

Bass   **Tenor**

☺☺☺☺☺☺☺☺☺☺☺☹

☺☺☺☹☺☺☺☺☺☺☹☺

☺☹☺☺☺☺☺☺☺☺☺☺

Soprano   **Alto**

Time for a reality check. Though intended to be helpful, this schematic is not a panacea. Before you get all worked up about it, realize that a few of your volunteer choristers will miss some rehearsals and some Sundays. This invariably will spoil your seating chart, so learn to deal with a well-intended but imperfect world. Let me relate an anecdote. At a recent conference, while I was giving handouts containing an outline of this chapter to people as they arrived, one woman stood up suddenly. She took one look at the handout and said loudly, "This doesn't apply to me! I only have eight people in my choir!" And she left. Well, she deprived us of an opportunity to share this "gospel" with her little flock. Your choir may react similarly and say, "This won't work for *us*!" The principles enunciated above are musically and acoustically valid. However, you will have to be the final judge of when, if, and how you can implement them for your choir.

Balance, Blend, and Ego

Balance denotes the relative loudness of one section with respect to another. Blend denotes the relative uniformity of individual sounds in a section or the whole choir. Ego means: "Well, what's it to you! I have a lovely voice and I'll sing as loudly as I please." These three are interrelated, of course.

One of the reasons I audition my university touring choir is to assure a reasonable chance at numerical balance among the sections. I have never auditioned a church choir but rather accept all singers who wish to join. If you have too many sopranos and too few tenors, for example, it is more difficult for the choir to sing in balance. If, perhaps, the fifteen sopranos would kindly sing more softly and the two tenors a more loud-ly—ah, then blend goes out the window. Nevertheless, to get a good sound it is necessary to strive for a decent balance among the voice parts. If everyone were conscious of not singing loudly as a general rule, two things would happen. First, choirs would achieve balance more easily. Second, blend would be enhanced. I'm not referring to timid singing. Far too many choir members pay less heed to their individual dynamics than they ought to. The director is ideally situated in front of the choir to assess dynamics, individually and by sections. Don't be afraid to assert control over the choir's balance. It is all too easy in rehearsals for the director to be engaged in listening for pitch and rhythmic accuracy, to be playing the accompaniment, and the like, and to allow matters of balance to handle themselves. Then, what a surprise! When it comes time to sing in worship, the choir engages in a shouting match rather than per-forming a beautiful anthem. You must always concern yourself with bal-ance. The ability to listen (*Figure 6*) is a shared responsibility by singers and director, but you have the final word in the matter. Exercise it. You may not be able to (nor wish to) regulate the number of singers in each section, but you must select repertoire wisely on the basis of the balance you can realistically achieve with your choir. For example, I wouldn't suggest "A Faithful Shepherd Is My Lord" for SATTBB with fifteen sopranos and two tenors in the choir.

You can develop blend most easily by working for uniform vowel sounds. Think of vowel sounds in two ways: the quality of the same vowel sound by all the members of the choir (singing "Ah," for exam-ple), and the quality of the sounds across the vowels. Does "Ah" spread sideways in the mouth, "Oh" go north and south, and "Oo" recede into the back of the mouth? Each vowel has a characteristic sound (too many choirs make all their vowels sound like "Uh") but the relative "bright-ness" or "darkness" of the various vowels should stay pretty much the same within a piece of music. Sometimes the style of the music demands a wholesale brightening or darkening of all the vowels throughout the piece, but sounds should not "jump" at you from word to word because they are sung with an odd assortment of vowel sounds.

There is a healthy expression of ego that exudes confidence. Unhealthy ego makes a singer's voice stick out in a crowd. Someone asked a prominent conductor what to do about that soprano with the loud voice in his choir. The conductor thought a brief moment and replied, "Alienate her!" Perhaps not a satisfactory answer for the church choir but one borne of repeated confrontation, no doubt. When a situation of this sort arises, it will test all your diplomatic skills. There is always a chance that loud singing comes from improper vocal technique; a little coaching might cure it. However, if the offending chorister has an attitude problem, you have to deal with the attitude for the sake of the choir. My mother used to say, "Use a little *psychology* on them." My mother never directed a choir, but her point was valid. Finding the cause is essential, but don't immediately assume the worst motives. However, Mr. or Mrs. "Big Voice" can do a lot of damage to rapport and to the ministry in which the choir is engaged.

Musical Styles

Much of the music your church choir sings is what we call *homophonic* music (literally "same sound"). Homophonic music is chordal in nature, like a simple hymn harmonization. In *homophony* all the parts move with the same or nearly the same rhythm, giving the sound of chords moving along with a tune in the top part. (In men's music the tune can be frequently heard in the second tenor or baritone.) We call chords the vertical element of music. *Homophonic* music has its counterpart in *polyphonic* music ("many sounds") in which each of the voice parts is essentially an independent melody. Harmony or chords arise from the coincidence of notes in the parts that move horizontally. Though not confined as a compositional practice to the Renaissance and Baroque (15th through mid-18th centuries), polyphonic choral music was widely prevalent then.

Because of its chordal nature, homophonic music can be made to sound more beautiful easier than polyphonic music. If you are building a sense of balance and blend, select something chordal to sing. You can turn your attention to intonation (tuning is easier when all the parts sing pitches of a chord at the same time), to dynamics, to articulation, and so on more easily in homophony than polyphony.

Should your choir develop a "sound?" I am a believer that the sound of the music derives from the style in which the music is written. One-size-fits-all choral sound is anathema to me. In the past there have been several prominent choirs that strove to develop a unique and identifiable "sound." By so doing, they tended to only program literature that sounded effective with their particular sound. This was a limiting factor. You would do better to try to discover from the music itself what sort of sound your choir needs to make to perform each piece authentically.

The best advice I can give a novice about choral sound is to try to imagine the sound of the music in the inner ear with as little assistance as possible from the piano. This is difficult to do, especially at first, but learning how is very advantageous. If you can, sing all the individual parts yourself in the context of your own range. Pianos are percussive whereas singing is sustained. If you need to "plunk out" parts to learn the score or to teach parts to your choir, play with the most musical, lyric, singing tone possible, unless of course the piece is supposed to be highly rhythmic and bouncy. Perhaps you can use a flute stop on the organ or have a flautist play the parts for you, regardless of the octave. The best way to teach what you want the choir to sound like is to model the part with your own voice, never mind your singing skills. It is the singing *style* that matters most. Obtain recordings of good choirs and listen to how they sing. Better choirs make a stylistic distinction from piece to piece. More mediocre choirs sound the same on everything they sing. Imitating excellent choirs that get it right can enhance your choir's sense of style.

Chapter 4
Rehearsal Is the Key

Success is spelled one letter at a time: "r-e-h-e-a-r-s-a-l." Upon occasion your choir will sing more beautifully on Sunday than at any prior time in rehearsal. Please don't rely on sudden inspiration for work that wasn't done in rehearsal. Many years ago I read a joking reference somewhere that the word "rehearsal" derived from the root for "rehash." While it is true that we need to repeat the same music many times for our choirs to learn to sing it beautifully, the process need not be as deadly as the word "rehash" suggests. In fact, some of the more aesthetically pleasing and inspired moments for choirs occur in rehearsals, wonderful moments that the choir and director would like to capture and release in small doses over time to savor again and again. Rehearsals can be fun and productive simultaneously. Indeed, I think they must be. If they are not, you will not have to worry long. Your choir will quit coming.

Planning

Effective, joyful rehearsals originate in the mind of the director. They must be planned. Spontaneity has its place in a rehearsal, but living in constant spontaneity is living in chaos. This is not to suggest that all rehearsals go according to plan or that you do not have to think on your feet at times. However, if you want to get something valuable accomplished on a regular basis, you must plan. Perhaps you will say, "Oh, but I have such an *artistic temperament*. What you are saying sounds so—so *mundane!*" My reply is, "You are not being 'artistic.' You are merely *disorganized*." True artistry requires discipline; skills do not develop overnight. Skills need to be practiced, and practice takes planning.

The choir director needs to make both long-range and short-range plans. Let's save the long-range planning for chapter 6. For discussion purposes, let us assume a scheduled rehearsal time and date, and that we have already selected the music to rehearse. What, then, does a director need to do to prepare for a rehearsal? Consider the following:

Assess the pieces to be rehearsed, determining
>how many pieces you can rehearse;
>how much time you can spend on each piece;
>which piece or pieces you can drop, if you must;
>the opening piece;
>the closing piece.

Study the music to be rehearsed, and
>develop a concept of the sound of each piece;
>identify potential trouble spots;
>have a plan to advance each piece in progress;
>have a plan to introduce new music;
>practice conducting/playing the accompaniment as needed.

Consider non-music matters, including
>routine choir business;
>important announcements;
>opening/closing devotions or prayers.

As you can see, this plan appears formidable already. Even veteran directors—perhaps I should say *especially* veteran directors—spend more preparation time before the rehearsal than time actually rehearsing. In order to give some concrete tips to you about how to rehearse effectively, I'm going to make up a list of music to be rehearsed with a fictitious adult choir next Wednesday evening from 7:30 PM until 9:00 PM at St. Amphibilus Church. Note that there is a dynamic shape to rehearsals which I have creatively termed "Beginnings," "Middles," and "Endings." Ninety minutes seems at first glance to be a long rehearsal, but it will be over before you know it—and even more quickly if you are oblivious to shaping the rehearsal. *Figure 11* lists the music to be rehearsed along with a few musical details. The titles are in alphabetical order. To spare you additional concerns, let's assume you have a capable accompanist and flute player, both members of the choir, who will be prepared to play and will arrive on time to the rehearsal. Additionally, they are really nice people to work with.

Figure 11
Hypothetical List of Music for Next Wednesday's Rehearsal

Hymn: "From All That Dwell Below the Skies" (stanza 2 for choir with organ)
Introit: "Psalm 34" for Sunday (SATB *a cappella,* includes unison chant)
"It Is Well with My Soul" (SAB with piano)
"Lamb of God" (SATB choir, flute and organ)
"O Clap Your Hands All You People" (SATB with organ)
"Psalm of Praise" (three-part men's voices with piano)
"With a Voice of Singing" (SATB *a cappella*)

What follows is a sample of my typical process in preparing for a rehearsal. The first thing I do is determine what *must* be known by Sunday without fail. In this case, there are two selections; the introit and the choir stanza of the hymn selected as the Hymn of the Day (*de tempore* hymn, or the "sermon hymn"). Additionally, I have selected "O Clap Your Hands" to be sung between the Old Testament and Epistle readings. If we absolutely must, we can postpone this piece a few weeks, but since its text directly relates to the Old Testament reading, it would be better to sing it this week. The list may strike you as quite a bit of music, but the hymn stanza is a simple arrangement, and the choir has previously sung psalmody of this type. Besides, we introduced "Psalm 34" in rehearsal last week. We also have been rehearsing the anthem, "O Clap Your Hands" for three weeks. We will need "Lamb of God" during Communion the following week, "Psalm of Praise" (men only) for the week after and both "With a Voice of Singing" (a fairly demanding piece) and "It Is Well with My Soul" for two weeks after that. (We have a Sunday off in there.) In other words, these pieces extend over a five-week period. I recall that we have rehearsed everything at least once and the most current pieces several times. Now I can establish an order for rehearsing.

We usually begin with an opening devotion and conclude with prayer. Choir business is minimal, but we must announce the choir social coming in two weeks at Mr. and Mrs. Friendly's house. Taking out my trusty legal pad I form a chart that looks like the following, *Figure 12.* Note: *I write down my plan; I do not trust my memory.* Committing the plan to paper makes me evaluate whether I can live with my decisions or not, and it *holds me to my plan* in rehearsal. Using the legal pad, I place timings in the far left margin, titles to the right of the double vertical lines on every third line. This arrangement gives me room below each title to make special notations about places to rehearse (e.g. alto part on p. 3,

42

third and fourth meas., and bass entrances on pp. 2 and 6). Since I have a chalkboard in the rehearsal room, I arrive early to jot down the timings and titles in rehearsal order, and maybe page references or special places to rehearse, but no other details. The rehearsal begins *promptly* at 7:30 PM.

Figure 12
Rehearsal Chart for Wednesday

7:30–:35   1.   Opening Devotion – based on Psalm 117
                    Segue to the hymn stanza, which is based on Psalm 117

:35–:45   2.   Hymn: "From All That Dwell Below the Skies"
:45–8:00   3.   Introit: "Psalm 34"

8:00–:15   4.   "O Clap Your Hands, All You People"
                    Note alto part on p. 3, third and fourth meas./bass entrances on pp. 2 and 6
                    Spot check beginning and ending/run through
:15–:25   5.   "Lamb of God"
                    Tune flute to piano
                    Check choir parts and dynamics pages 5-6/run through with flute
:25–:35   6.   "Psalm of Praise"
                    Assign a baritone to 2nd tenor last measure at the *divisi*
:35–:45   7.   "With a Voice of Singing"
                    Bottom p. 3 meter change/last page soprano "G" and 4/4 measure
:45–:50   8.   "It Is Well with My Soul"
                    Read through/drop if more time needed

For Sunday
:50–:53   9.   Introit: "Psalm 34"
                    w/o stopping

:53–:57   10.   "O Clap Your Hands, All You People"
                    w/o stopping
                    Reminder about choir party at the Friendly's house in 2 weeks
8:59   Closing Prayer

Rehearsing: Beginnings

The Eleventh Commandment: "Thou shalt start on time and end on time." You can adjust times to suit the choir's needs, but once a starting time is announced, *start on time*. Years ago, a popular family TV show ended at 7:30 PM, and many of my choir members watched it. Then we changed rehearsals to start officially at 7:40 PM and run until 9:10 PM. There is no reason you and the choir cannot share pleasantries right up until the official beginning time, but when the announced beginning time arrives, start the rehearsal no matter who is not yet present. Then go about the rehearsal as you planned and make no fuss over latecomers. If they had a valid reason to be late, they will come in quickly and get right to work. If they did not, why would you want to take choir time to fuss over them?

Begin your rehearsal with an *opening routine*. It can have weekly or seasonal variations, but establish a routine. My preference is to begin with a devotion that also incorporates singing a hymn. This way all minds and hearts can be directed to the task at hand and voices warmed up at the same time in a gentle way. Devotions may be lead by the director or choir members with a schedule planned in advance. The point I'm striving to emphasize is to establish a starting routine that sets a business-like tone and has a devotional quality.

If you prefer to begin with some vocal warm-ups, this is fine, too. I have placed information about warm-ups in chapter 8 under "Teaching the Choir," since I believe effective warm-ups have a didactic function. Ineffective warm-ups that are done in a routine manner often don't engage both the voices *and the intellects* of the singers, and generally accomplish very little. Some directors complain about the same few choir members who come ten minutes late to every rehearsal and miss the warm-up. Upon closer examination, we often find that these choristers believe the warm-up to be a waste of their time; so they arrive when they think the rehearsal will get down to business. I have observed far too many rehearsals that begin with talking and joking around, generally wasting ten minutes or more of time that could have been productive. Fifteen minutes of wasted rehearsal time each week throughout a choir year adds up to ten or more hours of lost rehearsal opportunities—*five hours accumulated in the weeks before Christmas alone.* Try not to waste time at the beginnings of rehearsals.

Generally avoid a lot of talking or doing business at the beginning of a rehearsal. This is a sure-fire way to misfocus everyone's attention and waste time. You'll have to reiterate the announcements at the end anyway, because nobody will be taking notes at the beginning. To review: start on time; start with singing, a prayer, or a devotion, but *start on time.*

Rehearsing: Middles

On the heels of the beginning of the rehearsal comes the music for the next time the choir sings publicly. Note in the chart above there are three items: an *introit* (this does not rhyme with a big city in Michigan; it is pronounced "in-TROH-it"), a hymn stanza, and an anthem to be sung between Scripture readings. Notice how I have included the hymn stanza in the opening devotion as a way of teaching about the text, warming up the voices, and rehearsing the hymn, all in the span of the first fifteen minutes. I have allotted fifteen minutes each for the introit and anthem. Because we sang them both in earlier rehearsals, they will have accrued about a half hour to forty-five minutes of rehearsal time each. If we have practiced effectively in previous weeks, fifteen minutes this week should be enough. If we need a few more minutes for either piece, we'll have to steal time from number eight in our plan, "It Is Well," since it is the least imminent to be performed.

Keep a good rehearsal *pace*. This is essential to a successful rehearsal. You need not be frantic; in fact, a relaxed pace may be all the traffic will bear. Pacing your rehearsal means keeping it moving without wasting time. Since you have listed the selections in order on the chalkboard, singers have no cause to wonder what piece is next. In fact, you can habituate their getting music in rehearsal order as they take their seats before the beginning time. Even if there was no time for them to do it then, no one should be in a quandary for long as to what is happening when you have recorded the rehearsal order for all to see. The more you try to estimate the length of time to spend on a piece, the better you get at estimating. Hold yourself to those timings, however, or you will never learn how to rehearse efficiently. If you truly need more time for a piece, use it, but don't let yourself off the hook too often. Be your own best time management critic.

The two biggest time wasters in a rehearsal, other than not starting promptly, occur between pieces and between rehearsing one section of the choir and bringing in the other parts. This is where maintaining the pace matters most. *It is vital to keep most of the choir singing most of the time.* For example, ask them all to sing one another's parts, so long as they don't fumble around badly and create another problem. If your choir has not rehearsed like this before, it may take some patience on your part to introduce it. Also, not everyone will be successful the first few times, so please don't give up too soon. Tough it out a little when they make mistakes. This technique has many significant advantages: stronger music readers in other sections will help weaker readers learn their parts; everyone's sight-reading skills improve over time; the choir develops a feel for the whole piece by knowing what is going on in the other parts; everyone stays focused; and because they are actively singing, they will be unable to chat with one another or disturb the choir.

Occasionally the pace of a rehearsal bogs down because the director does not know exactly what to do next. You may be surprised to learn that veteran directors experience moments like this also. What to do? Pick a spot in the piece to sing, *any spot*. Then while they are singing you have bought a brief moment to think what you need to do next. Not incidentally you may find that you have intuitively selected the very spot that needed work.

It is unnecessary and sometimes a great waste of time to rehearse every selection from the very beginning. Did you ever notice how many choirs know *beginnings* of pieces extremely well? If only there would have been *one more rehearsal* to learn the last two pages better! Suggestion: find a place where the choir is having difficulties and start near there. This needs to be a place where the choir hears the tonality of the piece easily. You can waste time and frustrate the choir by just diving into a tricky spot without some context. One of the most helpful contexts for the choir is having a firm sense of the key the piece is in at the point they begin singing. Ask your accompanist to play a few measures ahead, establishing the key so that the choir is prepared to enter with greater accuracy. Always set the sound of the piece in your singers' ears. That's what an introduction to a piece does. If you start in the middle or near the end of a piece, you must give the singers an introduction there too.

Many times you can use to your advantage a technique I call "reverse rehearsing." Suppose the selection is six pages long and somewhat regular in structure. If you start, say, in the middle of page 5 at a logical place and sing to the end, then when you start at the top of 4 and go to the end you will have *covered the ending twice*. Next, begin at the bottom of page 2 and go to the end, or maybe only as far as overlapping the place you first started. Finally, sing from the beginning, which is usually the easiest section of the music to learn. By using this procedure, you will have covered the middle and the end of the piece more often than the beginning. Your choristers will have gained a sense of where the piece leads so that they are not always plunging into unknown territory. In strophic pieces, such as hymn settings and Bach chorales, in which the music remains the same but the words are different, begin with stanza 3, for instance. Some musical problems arise in the simplest of settings because the choir is unfamiliar with the text.

I wouldn't apply the "reverse rehearse" procedure to every piece in every rehearsal, but it is a very useful teaching device. In *Figure 13* you can see I had already intended to do something very similar in my rehearsal plan by beginning with known problem spots (note the **bold italics**). Why spend the time singing through all the places in each piece the choir already knows well, leaving the important rehearsal spots until last? Occasionally isolate problem places, fix them, and *then* sing from the beginning.

Figure 13

8:00–:15	4.	"O Clap Your Hands All You People" ***Note alto part on p. 3, third and fourth meas./ bass entrances on pp. 2 and 6*** ***Spot check beginning and ending***/run through
:15–:25	5.	"Lamb of God" Tune flute to piano ***Check choir parts and dynamics pages 5–6*** /run through with flute
:25–35	6.	"Psalm of Praise" ***Assign a baritone to 2nd tenor last measure at the divisi***
:35–45	7.	"With a Voice of Singing" ***Bottom p. 3 meter change/ last page soprano "G" and 4/4 measure***

Two final suggestions for improving the efficiency of the rehearsal: develop a method to identify places in the music to which you wish to direct your singers' attention quickly, and use command words. Both deal with pace.

"Please start where you sing 'Lamb of God,'" you say.

"Fine!" they reply. "*Which* 'Lamb of God' did you have in mind?"

It is better to say, "Please begin on page 4, top score, second measure," or "Begin with the sopranos, measure 46." The more precise you are and the more consistent your method to identify places in the score, the more efficient your rehearsal becomes. "Two measures after rehearsal letter 'A' " applies to music that has sectional rehearsal letters. "Begin at the *pickup* note to measure 17" works well for many English language texts because English is primarily iambic, having many words that begin with unaccented first syllables. These will occur right before a downbeat, hence on a pickup note. Many musical phrases begin with an upbeat or pickup note.

In a difficult selection, there are times that you will have to start three or four measures before the actual place that needs rehearsing. That way, if there is an awkward entrance, it doesn't matter so much. Don't stop. By the time the singers get to the place you planned to rehearse, they will be fully singing their parts. There are times when it seems impossible to find a likely place to begin. When I find myself in a situation like this, I will go to the top of the page or the beginning of a line far enough in advance of the place to be rehearsed and start with whatever notes every-one has, regardless of phrasing. This particularly occurs when rehearsing polyphonic music.

If you work with an accompanist who has a score different from the choir, you may need to give the accompanist and the choir each a refer-ence peculiar to their scores, unless you use specific measure numbers. "Start at the top of page 5" means absolutely nothing to brass or string players, who play from a single line part with only measure numbers. "Start at measure 24" is clear to everyone.

Command words save time. A simple "Again!" communicates so much better than a sequence such as this: The director stops the choir and says, "Okay. That was pretty good but you can do better. So, let's go back and do this part over. Start where we just started. Yes, that's right—we're beginning again on page 5 at the top. Okay, can we have pitches from the piano? Good! Are you ready now?"

Yikes!

Command words work especially well if said in the tempo of the piece to maintain the beat. If you can do this, you will probably *not* have to stop to give pitches nor reestablish the beat—both time wasters. Fifteen seconds every time the choir stops adds up to a lot of wasted time by the end of the rehearsal. (For fun—or more likely for its shock value—have someone keep a stopwatch on the actual amount of time spent in your rehearsal singing, as opposed to talking or general down time.) Other command words might you employ include the following: "Higher/lower," "louder/softer," "faster/slower," "Tenors, come in," "E-

flat!" You can determine when to use them, or make up some new ones for yourself.

Rehearsing: Endings

Some rehearsals run out of time and stop, and some run overtime and fizzle out by attrition when members get up to leave. Neither is good. Remember the Eleventh Commandment: "Thou shalt start on time *and end on time.*" If you have planned your work and worked your plan, it will feel natural to you and the choir. End rehearsals by singing through one final time the selections for your next worship service, with a short announcement or an item of business if necessary, and a prayer, hymn, and/or the Benediction. Then stop. Only now has it become social time, if that's what you and the choir wish to do, because the work is finished and everyone feels a great sense of accomplishment and wonderment that the time passed so quickly.

Just as it is important to have a beginning routine, it is wise to establish an ending routine. It needs to take place regularly to bring proper closure to your rehearsals, even if you must break off doing whatever you had otherwise planned (such as "It Is Well"). Always leave the requisite time to do all of the closing routine. Choirs experience a sense of incompleteness or frustration with rehearsals that run right up to closing time and then stop abruptly without completing all the work originally planned. Round off the ending with a closing routine and leave the choir with a sense of completion. It is positive for them to yearn to get back to rehearsal next week to finish what was left undone and, at the same time, to feel a sense of completeness and accomplishment for what *was* done well.

Singing for Worship

Fifteen minutes of rehearsal time is necesary, even if there is only one small piece to be sung. A Sunday morning choir reality: three people running in from ushering, two from teaching Sunday school, and others bailing from the family car pool. Once again, the choir director needs to plan for this mini-rehearsal and work as efficiently as possible within the time available. Start on time, regardless of who is there. Since the worship service will not wait for you, you know you must end the preparation on time. It may not be possible to sing through each piece in its entirety. If you sing only specific measures and entrances, make certain that they are sung satisfactorily. When there is a tricky spot which worries the choir and you and there isn't time to sing it through well, you may be better off to sing only the beginning of the piece, smile broadly at the choir, and say, "Oh, you started this piece *so well* this morning. I know it will be *lovely!*" Your attitude during the Sunday morning preparation sets the mood for the entire morning. Be positive and upbeat; there is no alternative. End with a brief prayer, commend the choir's ministry this morning into the Lord's hands, and then go joyfully to sing in worship.

Looking Ahead

This week's rehearsal and Sunday morning singing are history. Now what? If you have the opportunity to do so before they all leave church, by all means tell the choir, "Thank you." Even if they didn't sound like the angels in heaven, they deserve to be thanked. If they weren't very good, or even as good as you thought they could be, you cannot in honesty tell them, "Great job!" But you can and should thank them for their hard work and fine spirit. There is always some poor fellow who worries aloud that he missed a note or two on page 5 or something like that. Ask him to estimate how many notes there are in the whole piece and then ask him how many he sang *well*. Remind him that players get into the Baseball Hall of Fame with lifetime batting averages under .300. His .985 "singing average" is an admirable accomplishment. (I'm serious—I use this imagery, and it really communicates.) So you missed *one*, did you? Statistically insignificant, I'd say. Oh, and try to avoid *post mortems* next Wednesday evening. Look ahead, not back.

Whether given to you directly or to the choir, words of appreciation from the members of the congregation should be received humbly and graciously. "Aw-shucks-It-was-nothing" or "We-really-didn't-do-so-well" kinds of responses are inappropriate. In a subtle but certain fashion, the first response denigrates the ministry of the choir and the second brims with false modesty. If you have a hard time receiving compliments—and some people genuinely do, unfortunately—you may literally need to practice responding "Thank *you*" or "You are *welcome!*" (spoken with a genuine smile). One of the marvelous features about ministry that keeps us humble is this: we never truly know what affect our music making has had on the faith life of any particular member of the congregation. I think God does this purposely so that we do not become depressed when we think we have failed nor conceited when we think we have done well. *"Soli Deo Gloria"* ("to God alone be the glory") is not an idle motto.

Then, planning for the next week begins. Three pieces move off your rehearsal chart, the next most imminent move up, and you add one, two, or three new ones to the bottom of the list. Try to stay four or five weeks ahead of performance dates, especially with adult choirs, because you know some members will probably be absent from rehearsals in the coming weeks. Five weeks rehearsing any given piece ought to be sufficient, unless you are preparing a major cantata or larger work. If it takes your church choir more than five good rehearsals to learn music well enough to perform publicly, evaluate whether you have selected music that is too difficult for them. If they can accomplish new music in only one rehearsal, they may be under-challenged.

Chapter 5
Conducting Basics

Music is sound in motion. It has a pulse called beat and moves at a pace called tempo. The director must convey these features to the choir, to an accompanist or accompanying instruments, and occasionally to the congregation when directing music that involves them. The primary way to do this is through a conducting gesture. Veteran conductors work for years refining their conducting techniques. A beginner can do a satisfactory job by knowing some of the basics of conducting, but it is important to improve conducting skills over time. First, we must consider some factors concerning motion in music, and then we can relate these to the conductor's gesture.

Motion in Music

When listening to songs over the radio or hearing a live performance in any musical medium, you can usually tap a foot in rhythm to the music. In fact, rhythm is one of the most obvious and universally compelling elements of music. All music conveys a sense of movement called the *beat*, the basic pulse of the music, distinct from the *tempo* or speed of the music. The rhythm of a piece is comprised of sounds that are the same as, longer than, or shorter than the beat. Rhythmic patterns make music interesting and pieces distinguishable one from another. "Beautiful Savior" has a different rhythm than "Amazing Grace." If we were to sing either of these hymns faster or slower, we would discover that the basic rhythms for each does not change with the change in tempo; they just sound faster or slower. A change in tempo does not alter the basic beat or rhythm, an important distinction. Sometimes choristers confuse these concepts and terms, especially younger singers.

Music that has a regular pulse usually also moves in regularly recurring accent patterns. That is, some pulses or beats are heard to be louder or more accented than others. This is termed the *meter* of the music. Music with irregular beat groups still contains meter. Since the accent groups vary, we refer to music of this type as having *mixed* meter. For now, it is easier to begin by discussing regular metrical organization.

Determining the Meter

In its simplest form, we may say that most music moves in groups of two or three beats, the first of which is accented. In the hymn examples already given, "Beautiful Savior" moves in accent groups of two beats, duple meter while "Amazing Grace" moves in threes, triple meter. In some music the meter is not easily identified. This is especially true if there are layers of rhythmic activity that distract our ears from clearly determining the basic pulse. In cases like these, one should attentively listen for any recurring accents, and try tapping a foot or counting "1 – 2" or "1 – 2 – 3" until what is done physically matches the sounds that are heard. Rhythmic concepts, the most basic of which is beat, are essentially physical concepts, not intellectual ideas. Though they can be defined verbally, they are often more satisfyingly described with bodily movement.

Printed scores use a *meter signature*, also commonly referred to as the *time signature*. *Figure 14* shows the most commonly used meters or time signatures. For uniformity, I have put these all on a G-clef, or treble clef, though the clef makes no difference regarding rhythmic notation. (Clefs determine pitch.)

Figure 14
Commonly Used Time Signatures

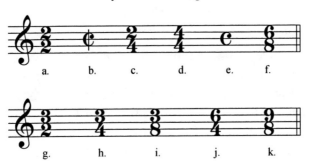

Examples *a–f* are *duple meters*; examples *g–k* are *triple meters*. Examples *a* and *b* are two different ways to write the same meter, sometimes called "cut time." Examples *d* and *e* are also two ways to write the same meter, sometimes called "common time." In examples *a, b,* and *g* the *half note* receives the beat. In examples *c, d, e,* and *h* the *quarter note* receives the beat. In example *i* the beat is the *eighth note* (though in faster music the beat is the dotted quarter). In examples *f* and *k* the basic beat is the *dotted quarter* (except in very slow music, when the beat is

53

the eighth note). In example *j*, the basic beat is the dotted half (except in slow music, when it is the quarter note.) We'll discuss the kind of conducting gesture (the hand and arm signals) necessary to direct these meters under "Beat Patterns."

Establishing a Tempo

Tempo is the pace or speed at which the beats occur. *Tempi* (plural of tempo) can be expressed in general mood terms, such as *"andante," "allegro," "presto"* and the like. These are Italian terms. Modern composers often use their native languages for such indications instead of Italian. Don't be surprised to see music marked *"lebhaft"* or "quick and bright!" The terms above and others like them only indicate an affective flavor and should never be considered definitive of precise tempi. Tempi may be accurately expressed in terms of beats per minute, such as "♩ = 84" or "♪ = 70–76". Sometimes affective terms and numerical markings are used in conjunction with one another. You may also see the numerical terms expressed "mm = 60," for example. This is a "Mälzel marking" or "metronome marking." (Though the device was actually invented in 1812 by Dietrich Winkler, Mälzel is the fellow who added a scale of tempo divisions, named, and *patented* the "metronome," thus becoming the target of a lawsuit. Ludwig van Beethoven memorialized Mälzel in a famous little canon and in the opening theme of one of his symphonies— interesting trivia to enliven a dull rehearsal.)

You can practice setting a tempo using either a mechanical or electronic metronome, or you can use a clock with a sweep-second hand to find a tempo (much like a nurse feels your pulse, watches the clock for ten or fifteen seconds, and then multiplies your heartbeat out to a minute). Of course, 60 beats per minute (mm = 60) is the easiest tempo to find in this manner. Since there are twelve large divisions in a complete minute (every five seconds), any multiple of twelve is also easy to find. In other words, three beats every five seconds equals 36 beats per minute. Four beats in five seconds equals 48; five equals 60; six equals 72; seven equals 84, eight equals 96, and so on. If you practice this a bit, you can select the most common tempi quite accurately in ten or fifteen seconds. You can interpolate between these more easily determined tempi easily, as well. My choirs know when I stare off at the wall clock for ten seconds I'm not hoping rehearsal will be over soon—I'm setting a tempo!

54

Always set the tempo firmly in your own mind before directing the choir or cueing your accompanist. When the piece begins with accompaniment, the director needs to establish the tempo for the accompanist (and know with confidence that the accompanist has grasped the tempo). I have witnessed many small disasters when a director allowed the accompanist to start the piece at her own tempo. Once the piece is started, the director, choir, and accompanist are captives to the tempo selected. Consequently, it is wise for the director to take a moment before beginning each piece to establish a suitable tempo. Re-read your director's job description. Establishing the tempo is in it.

Preparing the Choir to Start

Certainly, the director needs to set an appropriate tempo in preparing the choir to sing. The director also needs to give the starting pitches, convey the mood of the piece, as well as the style and timing of the breath, and indicate how loudly the choir is to sing. Many years ago I started a piece in a Christmas concert without giving the choir its opening pitches. Fortunately, they had rehearsed the piece so well that they came in relatively accurately out of habit. (Why didn't someone wave me off when I prepared to give the downbeat?) I could have avoided tempting providence had I thought to give the pitches first! Let me tell you, I don't do this often.

Giving Pitches

One may make a distinction between the manner of giving pitches in the flow of a rehearsal and in a performance. If you are not very subtle giving pitches in a rehearsal, nobody particularly will mind. On Sunday morning in worship, one needs to give pitches more discreetly. The most direct way to give pitches is to play them *gently* and *as musically as possible* on the piano. Two important items of advice: First, give pitches from the *lowest to the highest,* unless you play a chord containing all the pitches at once. This establishes the tonality for the choir, built from the bottom up. Giving pitches from the top down or at random is not an effective procedure. It is important that you teach your singers to conceptualize the sounds they plan to sing. Every chorister must have a firm mental image of the pitch, the quality of the sound to be made, the tempo, the dynamics, the mood of the piece, and so on. *Don't* permit or encourage your choir to hum the pitches back to you. Humming the pitch is musically distracting, and it is a poor way to establish the mental image required. It is an inherently unmusical practice. Humming also establishes a different vocal technique in the muscle memory of the singers than they need for singing (unless it is a humming piece). When they hum, many singers only approximate the pitch the director has given, or they establish a new and incorrect pitch. In other words, the director gives the pitch and then the choir gives twenty-five new pitches, each slightly different. If singers who are in the habit of humming starting pitches complain to you, be adamant. I am merciless when it comes to rooting out this practice. It is easy for the choir to adapt to the more productive and musical method of conceptualizing starting pitches if they abandon the practice of humming them as soon as possible.

In a rehearsal, if you or the choir feel in doubt about the starting pitch, it is better to have the choir *sing* the first note together *and hold it* briefly on the primary vowel of the first word as you evaluate whether the pitches are accurate. This procedure allows you to evaluate more than pitch accuracy. You can simultaneously judge the timbre of the sound, the balance and blend of the voices, the dynamic level, the articulation, and the precision of the initial attack very quickly. Having the choir sing a chord and hold it briefly anywhere in a piece that intonation or pitch accuracy is in question is a useful rehearsal technique.

As a young conductor I gave pitches to my choir by blowing into a *pitch pipe*, a practice I have long ago abandoned. (The sound of a pitch pipe has such suavity, beauty, and accuracy of tone—just *kidding!*) I used a pitch pipe in a concert many years ago. In this case the pitches the choir heard from me on the pitch pipe were augmented by a tiny voice in the audience off to my left spontaneously cooing in reaction to the pitches I blew. A little child, hearing the pitch pipe's metallic "toot" tried in his own way to imitate it. We might as well have guessed at the true starting pitch since now there were several "in the air." It was "every man for himself" for a few measures until the sound coalesced into a tonality acceptable to the more persistent singers. To be prepared to sing, the choir needs to hear one precise set of pitches given with clarity and brevity.

Basic Conducting Gestures

The most common conducting gestures a conductor needs to know are breathing gestures or preparatory beats, beat patterns, cues, and cut-offs. If conducting is new to you, at a minimum, consult a manual on conducting. Far better, observe a few good conductors in action (or watch some quality conducting videos), and take a class in conducting. You can learn so much more about conducting through *observation* than through reading.   For this reason, the next section may appear less detailed than you may wish. These are some basic concepts.

Breathing Gestures

Some conducting gestures are named for their functions. The *breathing gesture* is one of these. It should convey not only the depth and quality of the singers' breath, but also in the same motion convey the tempo of the music, the style and dynamic of singing, and the *timing* of the singers' breath to make the initial sound or "attack." For this reason, it is sometimes also called the *preparatory beat*. It is important to consider carefully the motion used to prepare the choir to begin. A breathing gesture that is out of character in any way with the music that is to follow will result in a sloppy or inappropriate beginning sound or attack from the choir. The director does not necessarily need to breathe with the choir but must at least simulate a breath in the proper style and tempo of the music. A director need give only one breathing gesture or preparatory gesture as a cue to the choir. Giving two or more preparatory beats, sometimes called a "double preparation," can be confusing and result in multiple entrances by the choir. The breathing gesture is always one beat before the music is to begin. If the singers need to begin on the downbeat, the preparation is the beat before, the upbeat. If the singers need to come in on beat three, the breathing gesture should be beat two, and so on. This holds true irrespective of the meter of the music or the beat pattern used. In most instances it is totally unnecessary and bad conducting technique to give beginning "dead beats"—that is, "1-2-3-4 - come in."

Beat Patterns

It is difficult to demonstrate something as fluid and three-dimensional as conducting gestures in two-dimensional line drawings, even with explanations. Furthermore, individual directors adapt the basic conducting patterns to suit their musical needs in particular places in a score. The best analogy that comes to mind is one of grammar in language use. In fact, a valuable conducting text by Max Rudolf has as its title "The Grammar of Conducting." The more extensive your vocabulary, the more varied your expression. However, nouns and verbs still maintain their proper functions. A conductor need not rigidly maintain the following basic beat patterns but will wisely glean from them the essential motions and the corresponding musical responses these motions elicit.

The most basic conducting pattern is one in which the motion is down and up alternately. A down motion conveys a point of arrival such as a stress or accent, and an upward motion conveys movement away from a point of arrival. We call these the "downbeat" and the "upbeat," respectively. Every beat pattern has one of each, although some patterns have beats between the down and the upbeats. Listed in *Figure 15* are the four most common beat patterns, showing both duple and triple meters. Notice that the upbeat in each case is not purely upward, but it is *upward and inward*. Notice, also, that in each case the downward motion of "one" shows a little *rebound*. In other words, the force of the downward motion is partially absorbed by movement to the side or slightly upward in a light bounce.

Figure 15
The Four Most Common Beat Patterns

58

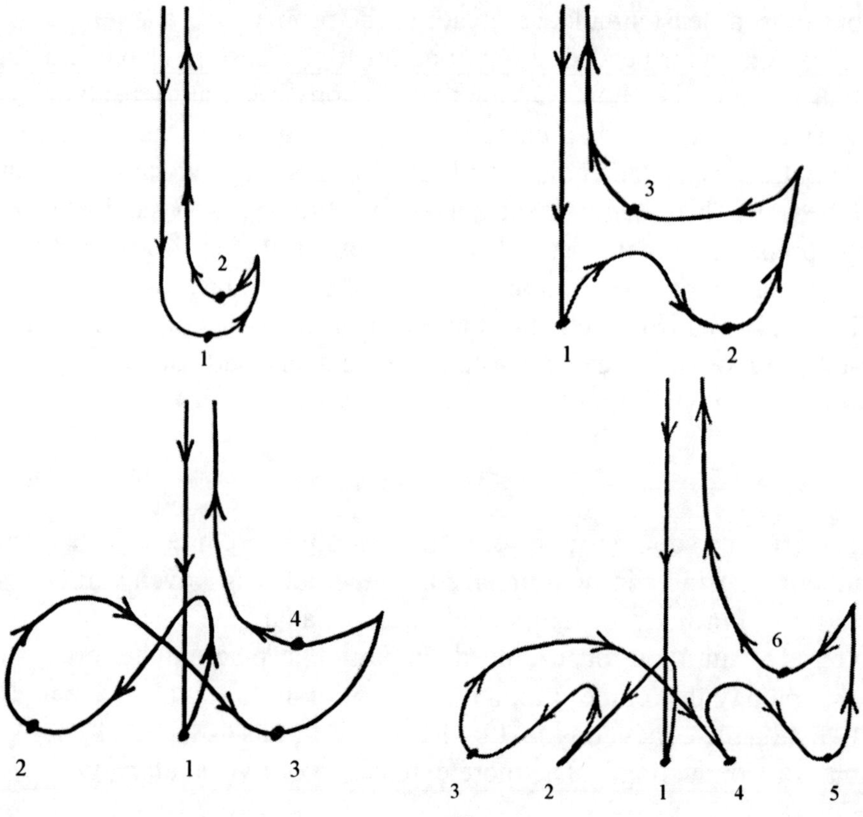

These patterns describe the hand motion of the conductor as the conductor faces the patterns. The choir will see them in reverse. For the "two" pattern, commonly called the "J-2," notice that beat two is almost in the same place as beat one, and the motion is (1) down and rebound slightly to the right, and (2) in and up. The "three" pattern moves (1) down with a slight rebound, (2) right with a slight rebound, and (3) in and up. The "four" pattern moves (1) down with a slight rebound up and right, (2) left and rebound slightly up and left, (3) across right and rebound a little up and right, and (4) in and up. The "six" pattern moves (1) down and slight rebound up and right, (2) down left with slight rebound up, (3) farther left with a rebound still farther left, and (4) across and down to the right but near the center line with a rebound slightly up and right, (5) down farther right with a slight rebound, and (6) in and up. Variations of these are common, and different conductors are certain to change their patterns dependent upon musical needs—a cue here, an accent there, a smoother articulation, a more pointed and rhythmic beat as needed. As a general rule, keep in mind that rebounds move either slightly up and/or in the opposite direction of the beat that is to follow.

The more fluid you can make your conducting gesture and the less wooden it appears to the choir, the smoother will be the singers' response. The sharper or more angular your gesture, the more rhythmic, accented, or precise the response. Ideally, larger gestures should elicit louder singing and smaller gestures softer. Routine use of large gestures denies the conductor control over dynamic variations and subtlety of expression in matters of rhythm, articulation, and line. Some conductors resort to larger gestures when their choirs experience rhythmic problems, often making the situation worse. When singers are not together rhythmically, it is more effective to use a smaller and more precise beat than a larger one, even though the intent may be to attract an errant singer's attention by means of a larger gesture. The easiest conducting gestures for the choir to see and to follow are those centered in front of the conductor's body, falling between the conductor's shoulders and waist. Keep your hands from crossing in front of your face so that your eye contact with the singers is never impaired. Economy of motion is important.

Try to keep the time between points of the beat pattern identical, unless you wish to vary the tempo. If your beats are erratic, the choir's singing will become imprecise and sloppy. If you wish to increase the tempo, progressively shorten the time between beat points, and *vice versa.*

Conduct the beat pattern with only one hand, your primary hand. Two-handed conductors look to me like they are dancing the hula if the patterns go in the same direction, or like windshield wipers if they go in opposite directions. A director needs to be able to effectively control the choir with one hand. I guarantee, if you truly can't be in control with one hand, using two hands won't be an improvement. The norm seems to be right-handed conducting, but if you are a natural lefty, there is no "law" that you must use your right hand for your primary conducting gesture. Clarity of expression matters most. If you conduct with your left hand, the beat patterns in *Figure 15* need to be reversed. When you use your left hand for a "two" pattern, beat one moves down and beat two moves in and up, though you may feel comfortable moving in the shape of a "J" down and outward a little to the *left*. For "three" patterns, movement becomes down, *left*, in and up. In a "four" pattern, beat one is down, two moves *right*, three moves *left*, and four is in and up. Finally, in a "six" pattern, beat one is down, two is right, three farther right, four across and left, five farther left, and six up and in. These patterns are reversed from those of a right-handed conductor.

Cues and Cut-offs

Conductors use a variety of motions to convey the starts and endings of the tone by their singers. The simplest cue or cut-off gestures are those given *on* a beat and are directed toward the person or section being cued. When possible, give the gesture while looking directly at the individual or group you wish to cue. If the entire choir is to come in or cut off at the same time, quickly survey the whole choir to gain their awareness that a cue is coming on the next beat. This is a visual preparation. In most cases, cues or cut-offs that come without warning don't achieve the intended results. The best way to give a cue or cut-off is to maintain the beat pattern, look directly at the person or section one or more beats *ahead* of time, and give a bit sharper impulse either for an entrance or exit on the appropriate beat. Conductors often use the non-beat pattern hand (usually the left) for cues. This takes some practice for beginners.

All conductors "swoop" at times when they should have "swiped." Until you feel entirely comfortable keeping the beat, it is very likely that you will lose your place in a pattern sometime while you are concentrating on another musical feature. If you get lost in the beat pattern, always remember "one" is down, and the preparatory beat for another pattern is up and in. You may safely circle the field with your hand for a moment before landing again to get yourself musically in synchronization. Just look "expressive" and nobody will criticize you! If you persist in directing with the wrong beats, you may encounter some rather interesting results.

Elaborate curly-cue cut-offs or pinching motions are unnecessary and sometimes elicit odd vocal reactions. Jabby little "clamping" gestures directed toward the singers are my least favorite cut-offs. I always imagine the conductor's hand doing that motion to my throat to make me stop singing. (*Gag!*) Simply give an accurate, pointed beat and expect the choir to stop with precision as well. This may be a classic case of "less is more" when it comes to gestures. You may have heard someone say, "It's in the *eyes*!" Whatever the conducting pattern, eye contact with the singers is essential for effective directing. If you look at your singers, you may properly demand that they look back at you just as frequently, especially at musically important places such as entrances and cut-offs. When the director and choir stare at their respective scores, the music suffers. If you hear yourself stressing repeatedly to the choir, "Look up. *Look at me!* " perhaps you need to give them something important *to look at*. Over time you can communicate more of your will to the choir through your eyes than through many hand gestures. *Eye contact* is the ultimate key to effective, expressive conducting. If a conductor's eyes and facial expression run counter to his or her hand and arm gestures, the choir is at odds over which to follow. Facial expression and eye contact can override conducting gestures. Not only is this true when these are in seeming opposition, but it is also true when dull, lifeless singing results, and a conductor shows a passionless, detached, uninvolved facial expression, though the conducting gestures themselves may be accurate and otherwise compelling.

Directing from the Keyboard

Capable keyboardists find themselves ensconced at the piano or organ in the dual roles of director and accompanist from time to time. They may find it difficult to distribute their attention effectively between directing and playing. Novice and veteran directors alike can fall into the trap of devoting their full energies to playing, largely ignoring the task of directing, and forcing the singers to fend for themselves. Though it may not be practical to have a free hand to conduct cues and cut-offs, and the occasional nod of the head is all that you can manage, try to make eye contact with individuals or sections for cues. Let me stress again, if you look at the choir, you have a right to expect them to look back. When you use a piano, if it is not possible for you to look over the top of the piano, you may be able to situate it sideways or on a slant to the choir so that you can see the singers at an angle to the right or left. I personally prefer to look at the choir to the right.

In situations where you must both accompany and direct, you may find it helpful to give some visual imagery to the singers by facial expression and preliminary conducting gestures before you sit down at the keyboard. This may help to establish the mood, tempo, and dynamics of the piece in the singers' minds before you, the conductor, also become the keyboard player.

Without fail, my singers sound significantly better when I haul myself out from behind the piano, look directly at them, and convey the character of the music and the sound I expect them to make by my facial expressions and conducting gestures, indeed, my whole physical posture and body language.

Chapter 6
A Matter of Accompaniment

The previous chapter ended with some suggestions for directors who served in the dual capacity of director/accompanist. This is not unique; many directors share these roles. Sometimes I lead the choir from the keyboard, but mostly I prefer not to do this, so that I can focus my full attention on conducting. Of course, that means I need to work with an accompanist. You may need to do so as well.

Working with Accompanists

Some church choirs are blessed with several excellent accompanists, and others scarcely can find someone to plunk out a few notes in a rehearsal. No one assisted me regularly as a keyboard accompanist with my previous parish choir, but I had a number of talented instrumentalists there to accompany the choir from time to time, including two sets of brass ensembles during the majority of my tenure there. I inherited a brass quartet of college-aged young men when I first arrived at the church, and I cultivated another quartet from beginning fifth grade players until they graduated from high school. Fortuitously, they began playing together just about the time the twenty-somethings started moving away! There were several violinists, a flute, and a clarinet player, as well.

Having a good accompanist to work with is a singular blessing. Working with a mediocre or temperamental one quite the opposite. Successful choir directors owe far more of their success than they may be willing to admit to the assistance of sensitive, faithful accompanists. Over time an accompanist becomes somewhat of an alter ego. Years ago with a community choir, I enjoyed a close working relationship with one fine pianist so familiar with my rehearsal technique that, when I stopped the choir, she gave pitches for exactly the place in the music she knew I wanted to rehearse without my saying anything. Wonderful!

Here are several tips to working with accompanists. Most accompanists appreciate knowing the repertoire to be rehearsed in advance. Not too many want to sight-read regularly in front of the choir. When you plan a rehearsal, provide your accompanist with the music as far in advance as possible, especially if the part is a difficult one. The same advice is *apropos* if you are planning a piece that uses instruments or handbells. Furthermore, when working with instrumentalists, it is prudent to keep a copy of each of the instrumental parts at hand so that a lost or misplaced part will not hamper a rehearsal or performance. All it takes is one missing trumpet part to scuttle a successful rehearsal or destroy a performance. Treat your accompanists kindly; they are not chattel, and in many cases they have *volunteered* to assist the choir. Even if they are paid, it is not unreasonable to thank them privately or publicly. Try to think of things that accompanists need to be successful, as if you were in their place, and *provide* it for them, e.g. music stands, an extra copy of the music for page turns, suitable chairs to sit on while playing, and adequate lighting.

Give directions to accompanists that make sense to them. Although pianists and organists frequently play from a choral score, instrumentalists usually do not. Thus, certain instructions like "start at the top of page six" have no meaning for them. At least learn to give locations in the score in terms that are clear and understandable to your accompanists. Every measure in a handbell part has a measure number, for example, which makes it easier to locate rehearsal points. A helpful habit to cultivate during your rehearsal preparation and score study is to identify likely places in the score at which you may start rehearsing if you have to stop to fix mistakes. Then mark in your score the kind of directions you can give to your keyboard player or accompanying instruments to find these places quickly. Once in a while a director needs to look at a violin or brass part in rehearsal when a question arises, but the director can minimize doing so through advance preparation. Running around looking at the instrumentalists' parts also undermines the credibility of the director in the minds of the players. A player may rightly think, "How can the director give me instructions if he or she doesn't know my part?"

Singing with Accompaniment

The most common accompaniments to choral singing are done with piano, organ, or electronic keyboards. There is a big difference both to your accompanist and to the choir when a change is made from a piano at rehearsal in the choir room to the organ in church. Unless the accompanist has made the tactile transfer from one keyboard to another, and the choir can imagine the sound of the performance instrument, it would be wise to have at least one final practice in the performance space with the performance instrument. It may mean something as simple as taking the choir to the sanctuary for ten minutes at the end of the rehearsal. Forgetting to do something so elementary may result in a significantly different performance by both the choir and accompanist.

Piano, Organ, or Keyboard

If you play piano or organ, you know what I mean about the "tactile" transfer from one keyboard to another. If not, you need to understand that it physically feels very different to play a piano, a mechanical (or tracker) action organ, an electric action organ, or an electronic keyboard. Some nuances that were worked out in rehearsal may completely disappear when the accompanist plays a different instrument. Not all piano music sounds equally beautiful or is even practical to play on the organ, and *vice versa*. Pianos are percussion instruments. Organs sustain sound. For this reason keyboard parts with arpeggios sound fine when played on a piano, but such musical figures may need to be modified into chords when played on the organ. It is easy to change dynamic levels quickly at the piano by playing more firmly or less so. This can be done in an instant, even on individual notes. In order to get louder or softer, organists must change registration (add or take away organ stops). A skilled organist can give advice about organ registration for accompanying the choir. If your organist is really a pianist in disguise, both of you may be at the mercy of a strange instrument. Then it is best to seek out advice from another organist, perhaps at a sister church.

Sometimes the sound of the organ *masks* the sound of the choir. That is, the sound of the organ covers up the distinct tone of the choir. Masking occurs most frequently when the organ is too loud, but it also occurs when flute and principal stops are too heavy in the choir's range. 8' and 2' stops may be preferable to two 8' stops or an 8' and 4' combination. Part of the reason organ sound more easily masks choral sound stems from the sustained nature of the sound of the organ that differs from both the timbre and the percussiveness of the piano. My experience has been that too many organists play too loudly when accompanying the choir. Organists who are not physically positioned to hear the sound of the entire ensemble, by habit may focus more on the organ. Furthermore, small organs may have only two or three stops that are effective for accompanying the choir. In an attempt to broaden this limited palette, an organist sometimes over-registers. When accompanied, the choir should never feel forced to sing louder than they are accustomed. The choir and accompaniment must work together as an ensemble in which neither sings or plays with inappropriate or uncharacteristic tonal quality.

Winds, Brass, and Strings

The majority of the instruments used to accompany church choirs are common band and orchestral instruments. Presumably you have some players available to you from the congregation. If you ask around a bit, you will be surprised at how many band instruments are stored in parishioners' attics and closets, waiting to be taken out of mothballs. Often, there are more soprano instruments available than anything else, and it is tricky to find or write effective music for a combination of two flutes, a clarinet, an oboe, two violins, and a trumpet all in the same piece. All of these instruments play more or less in the same range. *Figure 16* lists common instruments in columns by families and in rows corresponding to the standard four voice parts, SATB.

Figure 16
Common Instruments by Families and Approximate Ranges Compared to Voices

	Woodwinds	Brass	Strings
Soprano	Flute Clarinet Soprano Saxophone	Trumpet Cornet	Violin Oboe
Alto	Flute Clarinet Oboe Alto Saxophone	Trumpet Cornet French Horn	Violin Viola
Tenor	English Horn Bassoon Tenor Saxophone	French Horn Tenor Trombone Baritone Euphonium	Viola
Bass	Bassoon Baritone Saxophone	Tenor Trombone* Bass Trombone Baritone Euphonium Tuba (Sousaphone)	Cello Bass**

*Don't go below F   **Usually doubles the cello part an octave lower

Some of these instruments are *transposing* instruments. That means, given the same notes to play from, they will sound in different keys. I first discovered this phenomenon as a fifth grader, eagerly playing the melody of a hymn on my new trumpet with a friend playing the bass part on his trombone. I don't remember the name of the hymn, but I vividly remember it sounded like "Chopsticks" all the way through the hymn! My friend played a tenor trombone, which sounds in concert pitch. It is called a "C" instrument. I played a B-flat trumpet. To sound properly with the trombone, the trumpet part needs to be transposed. Transposition means writing a part higher or lower so that the sound comes out in the same key as concert pitch instruments.

C instruments play in concert pitch. Pianos and organs, guitars, flutes, oboes, strings at all levels, bassoons, trombones, bass clef baritones, euphoniums, and tubas are C instruments. Clarinets, trumpets, cornets, and treble clef baritones are B-flat instruments. They sound a B-flat pitch when playing a written C. Because they sound *a whole step lower* than concert pitch, you must write their parts *a whole step higher* to compensate. For a piece in C major, the trumpet part must be written in D major. For a piece in E-flat major, the trumpet part must be written in F, and so on. There are C trumpets that do not need transposition, but most players commonly use B-flat trumpets. A cornet is similar to a trumpet except that it has a wider bore (the diameter of the tubing is a little larger) and it can have a more mellow sound. Practically speaking, trumpets and cornets can be freely interchanged. (Treble clef baritones sound a major ninth lower than written, that is, *an octave plus one whole step.*)

The other most common instrumental transposition is that for the French horn (a brass instrument), which is an F instrument. That means when playing the written pitch C, the horn will sound an F, a fifth lower. If the piece is written in C major, the horn needs to read in G major, *a fifth higher*, to sound in concert pitch. French horn parts are usually written in treble clef. English horn is a double reed woodwind instrument, not to be confused with French horn. However, it transposes the same as the French horn. Both English horn and French horn are considered tenor instruments. (When players talk about playing a "horn," they refer specifically to the French horn and not to brass instruments in general. Though he may know your meaning, it is technically incorrect to ask a trumpet player, "Do you play a *horn* in the marching band?" "No," comes the reply. "I play a *trumpet!*")

Soprano and tenor saxophones are B-flat instruments, but alto and baritone saxophones are E-flat instruments. E-flat instruments sound an E-flat when playing a C. Therefore, they need to read an A-flat to sound a C concert pitch. And, they read in treble clef! Confusing? Keep one of many available pocket-sized booklets with transposition charts as a ready reference.

Percussion

Frequently used percussion instruments include triangles, cymbals, finger cymbals, tambourines, claves, rhythm sticks, guiros, sand blocks, wood blocks, field drum (a snare drum with the snares turned off), bass drum, tubular bells, and tympani (two or three to a set). Some of these are quite simple to play. For others, find a player with appropriate background to assist you. Speak to a local elementary or high school band director about playing techniques and availability of instruments. Wind and string players often own their own instruments, but people who play the larger or more exotic percussion instruments often play one owned by a school. Except for tubular bells and tympani, for which pitches are notated, percussion instruments read from a single line staff without a key signature.

Handbells

Many churches own a set of handbells or choir chimes. These range from two-octave sets up to five octaves and more. To play well, handbell choirs demand considerable dedication and practice time. Whereas a vocal choir can perform with even a few people missing, a handbell choir can be in dire straits with just one person missing. Occasionally, a piece of choral music calls for only five or six bells that can be rung by two or three people, usually no more than two bells per ringer. The same is true for choir chimes.

Bell players need a place to set down the bells on cloth-covered foam. An entire handbell choir uses several tables and takes up a considerable area. Bells must be arrayed from one end to another of the performance space. Players cannot stand behind the vocal choir or in a knot to one side or the other of the singers. If you are contemplating using an ensemble of bells, brass, the organ, two tympani, and the choir, you will need a large performance space to assemble all the performers. Although I have conducted pieces with handbells ringing in one location and the choir

68

singing from another, this physical setup is not ideal, nor is it generally convenient to have performers of any kind widely separated. In these situations, performers may see the conductor's beat but hear sounds at different times. Unless they compensate for the spatial differences when they are spread out, conductors and players alike have a difficult time keeping the music together rhythmically. I mention this particularly in conjunction with handbells because some churches place handbell tables in front of the first pews but situate the choir in the rear gallery of the church. A workable solution may be to direct both groups from the center aisle of the church at a point equidistant from each, although this can pose a visual distraction in worship.

It is usually best to have only one conductor for the entire ensemble rather than a choir director and a handbell choir director who watch each other and the organist in order to stay together. I have done the latter, but it takes tremendous coordination between the directors and the performers to be successful. In such a case, *one* of the directors must lead and the other directors must follow *exactly*. There is no room for individual variations in interpretation or tempi.

Handbells are transposing instruments, but the transposition is an easy one. Handbells sound an octave higher than the written notation. If you practice a choir/handbell piece on the piano and only later use bells, play the bell parts on the piano an octave higher than written to accustom the choir to the actual pitches of the bells. Sometimes it becomes necessary to substitute piano for the bells in performance. Then, because of the difference in timbre between piano and bells, it may be better to play the bell parts at concert pitch (exactly as written). Use your musical judgment in such cases to determine which octave sounds better on the piano.

Chapter 7
A Matter of Organization

At first glance, this chapter may seem rather eclectic, the only thread running through it being "organizing" things. However, as the chapter unfolds, I think you will see it progress logically. I suggested in chapter 4 that one cannot expect inspired singing to result regularly from unplanned rehearsals. What is true on a small scale is true on a large scale also. We have enshrined this notion in popular sayings: "Plan your work and work your plan." "You will reap what you sow." "Put all your ducks in a row!" Yogi Berra reputedly once said, "If you don't know where you are going, you're liable to end up somewhere else." Well, then, before we wear out our clichés, let's set some goals.

Setting Goals

Through years of experience I have found it convenient to split the choir-year goals into two parts: "fall season" and "spring season." In this way, I can focus the choir on getting the year *started*, September through Christmas, and later *re-started*, January through Pentecost (or the beginning of June). I don't neglect to set summer choir goals, but next summer is too distant and far too unpredictable for me to plan at the end of *this* summer. I'll set goals for next summer after next Easter at the earliest. That itself is a kind of goal: knowing when to formulate new goals, or, if you will, "planning to plan."

Goals need not be written in highly formal language, but it helps to write them down, group them, and establish criteria by which to judge if they have been achieved. Otherwise, how do directors know for sure whether they have arrived wherever it is they were going? What sort of goals do I set? *Figure 17* lists my ideas for the "fall season." The numbered items are broad goals. The sub-sets are narrower goals and ways to measure their achievement.

Figure 17
Goals for the Fall Choir Season

1. Build the choir's membership
    Find more choir members generally (4–6)
    Altos specifically (2)
2. Sing frequently in worship
    Sundays per month (minimum 3)
    Festival services (Thanksgiving, Christmas Eve, Christmas Day)
3. Select new music for the choir
    Introduce at least ten new pieces
    Minimum two per month and two additional at Christmas
4. Plan a "big production" for Christmas
    Choral vespers
    Use instrumentalists from the congregation
    Congregational participation
5. Involve the school choir with the adult choir
    Christian education Sunday
    Christmas season
6. Improve communication about worship
    Meet with the pastor monthly
    Develop an entire fall season choir schedule—update periodically
    Write choir "tidbits" monthly for church newsletter (web site)

Writing goals and writing *realistic* goals can be two different matters. To be sure, set high goals. Dream a little. Don't be crushed if you don't achieve everything, but evaluate the goals and the results objectively. Sometimes the goals were realistic enough, but the methods you used to achieve them were deficient. Other times, factors beyond your control came into play. Perhaps you wrote *too many* goals. It is better to set and achieve only three goals than to plan and fail to achieve a dozen. Without specific goals, director and choir can muddle along amiably in a "business as usual" mode and never break any new ground.

Looking over the list in *Figure 17* again, note that goal 1 deals with recruiting, 2 with scheduling, and 3–5 with scheduling, budgeting, and selecting repertoire. Goal 6 is a broad communications goal for the entire year, perhaps being an on-going goal throughout a director's tenure. With specific goals for planning, a director can set to work in each area to achieve each goal as the Lord blesses you with success.

Recruiting

"Recruit constantly!" I remember reading this advice somewhere over thirty years ago. Constant recruiting has various facets to it, however. It is one thing always to be on the lookout for new choir members and another to start every conversation with "*You* should be singing in the choir!" Use that guilt-laden line often if you want to have fewer conversations. Still, there is no better way to recruit than through one-on-one encounters. People don't readily respond to notices in church bulletins or newsletters such as this one: "New choir members welcomed! Come one, *come all!*" Ads like that are always meant for *someone else*. Perhaps the sentiment needs to be expressed, if only to create the proper aura. If a director stops there, however, recruitment will fall short of success.

Strategies will differ from parish to parish. In larger urban congregations where membership changes a fair percentage each year, it may be easier to stay on the lookout for new members. Even if new parishioners don't immediately commit to the choir, a director can keep track of them and have various choir members speak to them over time. Persistence pays dividends; a one-time contact rarely succeeds. In smaller congregations or more settled parishes, recruitment potential is limited. Despite that fact, continue to be on the lookout for new choir recruits.

Chapter 1 identified the issue of commitment. Directors need to be sensitive to the nature of the commitment they ask of new choir recruits. Personally, when someone approaches me to take on new duties at church or school, I wonder aloud if I am being asked to "sign on for life." Quantifying a trial period for people helps. A director who recruits "snow birds" must make allowances for the fact that they will miss a large segment of the choir year, the time of year depending upon whether they migrate north or south. If this is unacceptable, don't ask in the first place, and avoid the attendant disappointment or embarrassment when these singers leave. Few church choir directors regularly turn away new members because too many are flocking to choir rehearsals, however. Recruitment is a serious and on-going concern for veteran and novice directors alike.

What is your "schmooze factor?" Can you meet and talk with people easily? For some people "schmoozing" carries a connotation of being artificial, insincere, or political. I don't advocate being any of those at any time. You may detest chitchat. You may busy yourself with seemingly more important matters, leaving little time for conversation. You may be naturally shy and have a difficult time meeting new people. Perhaps you simply *must* rush home for Sunday dinner after the late service every week. However, the higher your visibility in the congregation, the higher your recruitment success is likely to be (and success with other matters as well). If you are diffident by nature, try one of these strategies. Start at the top of my list and work your way down over successive Sundays. Here is a sure-fire plan to meet people that will take you from Labor Day through mid-October if you are *really* shy! Otherwise you can work through the list in a week or two, at most (just a *little* tongue-in-cheek).

> *Hang around* in the narthex (or fellowship hall) between services.
> Stand in *the middle* of the narthex, not in the corner.
> *Smile* and *nod* at people as they walk by.
> Smile at them and *say*, "Good morning. How are you?"
> When possible, do this and *shake hands* with the other person.
> If you overhear a conversation about the weather, *join in.*
> *Ask questions* like, "Who is playing this afternoon?"
> *Offer comments* like, "Wow! How *about* those *Packers*!"
> *Be patient.* Sooner or later an opportunity to talk about the choir
>   will arise.

The bottom line is this: the director needs to be well-known by members of the congregation and appear to them to be *friendly and approachable.* Though people may recognize who you are, few will attempt to engage you in conversation if they don't *know* you personally. This, unfortunately, is a characteristic of human nature. More important, you will not know *them.* Interest yourself in other members of the parish and what they do, and they will in turn interest themselves in you and your work. This has broader implications for recruiting, scheduling, budgeting, and the like.

Scheduling

People are creatures of habit; and church choir members certainly pose no exception. New directors can benefit from knowing old choir routines. Sometimes it is best to follow the established routine, and at other times it is best to strike out boldly with a new plan. The context of the situation should give you the first clue.

If the goal is to have the choir "sing more frequently in worship," and the sub-goal is to sing "a minimum of three Sundays per month," then plan accordingly. Take a sheet of that legal pad purchased for rehearsal planning, the church calendar, a soft pencil with an eraser, and begin to plan. In the left margin, write the month and date of the first choir Sunday, followed every other line by the month's successive Sundays, until the next month and date, and so on, all the way to the end of December. Since Thanksgiving Day falls near the end of November, and three mid-week Advent services may occur shortly thereafter, make room for these originally, or insert them between the Sundays you have already listed. If your worship is liturgical, notate briefly the names of the Sundays or other occasions to be celebrated. This helps determine "must sing" Sundays for the choir and alerts you to occasions for which plans by the Boards for Evangelism, Stewardship, and Christian Education have implications. If you suspect local modifications to the standard liturgical year will occur, attend the church's planning meeting, speak with the pastor, call board chairs, or copy the information from the church newsletter. It will not do to plan for the choir season without considering the parish's specific plans. Note all of these matters briefly on the legal pad before writing down details for the choir.

Goal number 5, "involve the school choir with the adult choir," is a further factor to consider in scheduling. As minister of music, I accompanied the school children when they sang, but I did not direct them. Therefore, it was necessary to coordinate the singing schedule of the elementary school children with the adult choir schedule. One of the teachers and I met periodically to establish a combined singing schedule and work out any changes that developed. It was always an amiable process; the adult choir accommodated the infrequent changes in the school schedule easily, especially when these were known sufficiently in advance. (If there are several directors, it is essential to remain on good terms with all of them and be flexible.) The school children and the adult choir occasionally sang a combined number, a pleasure for both choirs and for the congregation. You need not wait until a festival occasion to do this.

Perhaps it can be surmised from my description that we held two similar services every Sunday, allowing the children to sing in one service and the adults on the other many Sundays of the year. If there is only one service per week and the church has several choirs, it may be unrealistic to set as a goal having the adult choir sing an average of three

Sundays per month. If there are parents of school-aged children in the adult choir, they may not wish to stay through two complete services on Sundays when their children sing, or it may be impractical for them to do so. When our children sang in the first service, I solved this dilemma by scheduling the adult choir in the second to sing between Scripture readings (which as a rule occurred about fifteen minutes into the service), excusing parents to leave quietly during the introduction of the sermon hymn. Choir members may be able to suggest solutions to some of these little problems if nothing workable leaps to your own mind. Here is a chance to put collective creative thinking to work for your mutual benefit.

There are a number of places within the worship service where choral singing is appropriate. Some choirs have "anthem-itis," a condition causing them only to want to sing an "anthem" for worship, sometimes in a spot labeled "special music." There are a number of reasons why I do not chose such an approach. First, the term "anthem" historically is an English term to describe a genre of music. Today one finds this term applied generically for almost anything the choir sings that doesn't have a liturgical name, such as *introit*, verse, psalmody, *gradual*, or one of the parts of the Ordinary. Choirs that sing only "anthems" limit their scope and function tremendously. Second, "special music" is the kind sung as entertainment at women's society luncheons or PTL meetings. Music in worship can be called "attendant music" because it attends the service, that is, it is integral to the themes and the action of worship. My father related to me that, many years ago, when it came time for the choir to sing, my great uncle David would say, "*Und* now the choir *vill* refresh us *mit* another song!" I hope the singing was genuine spiritual refreshment, but it sounds to me a little bit like a musical "time-out," the commercial break in an otherwise overly verbal program. The choir's singing *attends* the service rather than *intrudes*, even as it "refreshes!"

Even if the choir does not function liturgically, there are opportunities for the choir to sing in a variety of places in worship. Two important places are attendant to Scripture readings and during the distribution of Holy Communion. A choral selection may aptly prepare a Scripture reading or it may respond to one. Using a choral piece with the same text as the reading or from a parallel passage in Scripture highlights the reading. It permits the congregation to reflect more deeply on the reading by reiterating or providing commentary on the text.

The practice of choral singing during Communion is deeply rooted in the church's heritage. It offers an opportunity for the choir to provide music reflecting upon the meaning of the Sacrament, or for the choir to sing a Psalm, hymn, or "anthem" based on one of the day's Scripture readings (*pericope*), or to evoke an atmosphere of prayer and meditation by the worshipers at that point in the liturgy. If the congregation normally sings one or more hymns during the distribution of Communion, the choir may assist the singing by introducing a new hymn, singing alternate verses of a familiar hymn, or reinforce congregational singing during that time.

Quite by accident, I encountered an unusual situation years ago regarding the choir's singing during Communion services. During the week, the senior pastor approached me to ask how I determined the choir's singing schedule. It seems he had fielded a complaint from a member who "never heard the choir sing on Sundays." Our parish held two Sunday services each week, one a Communion service and the other a non-communion service, alternating from early to late every week. I carefully explained that, when possible, the choir was scheduled to sing during the Communion service so that the choir members could more easily commune. I didn't want to set them at odds with the parish's Communion schedule or force them to attend additional worship services. It turned out that the fellow's problem was not entirely that he was missing hearing the choir sing. In reality, he had a different and more important faith-related issue to confront.

Scheduling the choir to sing ought to be a more thoughtful process by the director than picking a choir piece and unloading it on the congregation when the choir seems ready. Part of the process is the selection and purchase of music for the choir. Being of a pragmatic nature, I prefer to consider the budgetary implications before we select the choral repertoire for the year.

Budgeting

A realistic budget is based on setting realistic goals for music purchase. The two ideas are inseparable, but unfortunately the availability of money drives the music acquisition process more often than the reverse. A choir may be able to supplement its regular budget by means of donations and memorials, but it should not have to expect these additional funds to stretch the annual choir budget. Expecting donations year after

76

year to supplement or even supplant the budget is a dangerous process. Over time, it teaches the congregation to undervalue the choir and its work. Suppose we adopt goal 3 for the fall season: "Introduce at least ten new pieces." What financial implication does this have for the choir budget? It is easy to show this in tabular form. *Figure 18* indicates the cost of providing music for choirs of modest size. You can extrapolate figures as needed. If the church is serious about building a music library, plan to purchase five to ten more copies of each new piece than immediately needed to cover replacement of lost or damaged music and to provide for additional choir members, should your first goal succeed. Don't forget to include in your figure copies for the conductor and accompanist and parts for the instrumentalists, when needed. Some titles become unavailable for purchase in succeeding years. They become "POP," "permanently out of print." If you need more copies of a title permanently out of print, it is not legal to run to the copy machine to provide them. It is necessary to contact the publishing house for permission to copy, pay any requisite fees for doing so, and then pay photocopying costs. In my experience, photocopies, when legal—*and most times they aren't*—generally do not stand up well over time anyway. Aside from the legal and moral implications, never consider photocopying to be a long-term financial solution to a small budget. Purchase a few extra copies originally and save yourself and the choir from this almost inevitable dilemma.

Figure 18
Budgeting for choir music purchases

Cost in dollars for new titles at $ 1.00 per copy
Cost in dollars for new titles at $ 2.00 per copy

Number of New titles:	1	5	10	15	20
Number of Copies per Title:					
10	10	50	100	150	200
	20	*100*	*200*	*300*	*400*
20	20	100	200	300	400
	40	*200*	*400*	*600*	*800*
25	25	125	250	375	500
	50	*250*	*500*	*750*	*1000*
30	30	150	300	450	600
	60	*300*	*600*	*900*	*1200*
35	35	175	350	525	700
	75	*350*	*700*	*1050*	*1400*

At the time of this writing, single octavo prices averaged closer to two dollars than one dollar per copy, excluding shipping costs. Setting a goal of ten new choir pieces for the fall (by extension, twenty new pieces for the entire year) will require a substantial outlay of funds. It is an unrealistic goal when facing a choir budget of only $300. ($300 realistically will purchase six to eight new titles for approximately 20 singers.) Remember, we established goal number 4, "plan a 'big' production at Christmas." The cantata you have your eye on at $9.95 per copy plus shipping will cost over $200 for a choir of only twenty singers. Subtract this amount from the total budget. As the saying goes, "*You* do the math."

Of course, a director must count on using music already in the choir library. It is unreasonable to expect to purchase entirely new music for every occasion for which the choir plans to sing. How often the choir may repeat repertoire from the library depends upon a number of factors, including the choir's patience to sing John Stainer's "God So Loved the World" three times every year for the foreseeable future. Even "war horses" need to be put out to pasture once in a while. We sometimes speak disparagingly of congregations that are in a rut with hymn singing as only knowing their "favorite fifty." Some choirs similarly *starve* for new repertoire.

Selecting Repertoire

In *Figure 17*, we established a goal for the choir to sing three times per month for nine months. To do so requires a minimum of twenty-seven titles without repetition. In the planning process, think ahead from September through the beginning of June and count the additional festival or occasional services for which the choir may sing. These may include some or all of the following: Thanksgiving Day, mid-week Advent services, Christmas Eve and Christmas Day, Epiphany, Transfiguration, Ash Wednesday, mid-week Lenten services, Maundy Thursday, Good Friday, Easter, Ascension Day, and Pentecost. Conservatively speaking, for the choir to sing on Sundays and for most of the occasions listed requires about fifty musical selections throughout the year, not an insignificant amount of repertoire. What repertoire shall the choir sing and how will you go about selecting it?

There is a theoretical answer and a practical answer to this question. Theoretically, you should consider the wide variety of repertoire available for the choir to sing:

Liturgical music
psalmody, *introits, graduals*, verses, offertories, parts of the Ordinary
Hymn-based music
alternate stanza settings, hymn concertati
Scripture-based anthems
Seasonal selections
General choral anthems

A varied choral repertoire from the genres listed offers several advantages. First, the parish's worship becomes rich and well-rounded, due to the choir's leadership in the liturgy. The choir develops a sense of being integral to worship, not peripheral by merely inserting an "anthem." Second, the choir may sing two or more selections on a Sunday, such as a Psalm or a varied hymn stanza in addition to a choral anthem. In this way, the efforts of the choir are maximized. If selections are repeated later in the year, such as can be easily scheduled during the distribution of Communion or during the gathering of the offering, the choir has opportunity to improve and sing the piece with greater nuance and subtlety the second time. Third, by varying the choir's repertoire, the director can program easier and more difficult selections alternately to give the choir the occasional "breathing room" it needs when grappling with a demanding schedule or dealing with absent choir members. For instance, if you know in advance that some important voices will be missing on a given date, schedule an appropriate hymn stanza, a Psalm, or something else suitable that the choir knows by heart. Finally, varying the repertoire creates opportunities to schedule instrumentalists, handbells, and accompanists more frequently than only at Thanksgiving, Christmas, and Easter. For example, psalmody effectively employs a few handbells or one or two instruments. This gives the music special appeal to the congregation on ordinary Sundays while enlisting parish musicians at other times of the year than those few pressure-filled and hectic festival seasons when every church is searching for players.

As you consider the many possibilities, plan a varied choral repertoire to include music from some or all of the categories listed. Then, become as familiar as possible with the choir files before you make new purchases. It has happened to me that I purchased music already on hand because it was misfiled. And I assumed we didn't have the title in the library because I couldn't find it. At fifty or more dollars a mistake, this is not one a director needs to repeat.

Now it is time to fill in the details remaining on your scheduling chart, noting the Scripture readings or themes for each of the occasions you have scheduled the choir to sing. Match your musical needs with the music on hand, determining new music purchases to fill in places where there are gaps or to enrich various occasions with a particularly appropriate new composition or arrangement. Done well, this is a thoughtful and time-consuming project. There is an art to programming for a choir year, and I have yet to find a short cut to the process. It need not be nerve wracking, but it can become so if the director doesn't begin the process early enough to avoid being pressured into quick decisions or decisions contingent upon receiving music from a supplier in sufficient time for proper rehearsal. Some directors wait until it is physically impossible for a dealer to deliver music in time to meet the director's rehearsal schedule, and then they blame the dealers for being slow. This is unfair to the dealers and unwise. Experience tells me that it is better to plan for a season all at once rather than on a weekly or monthly basis. This is true particularly when ordering new music.

There are some helpful guides available to assist you to plan. Many publishers suggest a list of choral selections for use according to the liturgical year. In their catalogs, some publishers include listings of Scriptural references upon which choir selections are based. Even if you do not purchase music from these catalogs, you can get ideas about titles appropriate to various Sundays in the church year from listings like these. Fortunately, if your church follows the Common Lectionary, you can determine all the readings well in advance. Scripture readings rotate on a three-year cycle in the Lectionary. Music wisely chosen for one liturgical occasion will also be appropriate for that occasion three years later. (Note, the readings for a few liturgical dates are the same *every* year.) If forced to choose among several desirable musical selections, a director may be comforted to know that the pieces left out of the current plan may be programmed in a succeeding year. Since hymn selections frequently are based on the Lectionary—true at least for the hymn of the day (the *de tempore* hymn, often called the "sermon" hymn)—choral variations of hymn stanzas or new settings of hymn texts can be effectively worked into the plan too.

Ordering Music

After you have determined the choir's repertoire, it is time to order new music. When ordering new music, always remember to allow for sufficient delivery time to be able to rehearse each piece effectively. It doesn't harm to have a "Plan B" for rehearsing in case there is a delay in shipment.

Ordering music is quite easy when all the appropriate information has been gathered. Neither your favorite music dealer nor publisher reacts kindly to sketchy information. You may receive something you didn't want if you order only by title. For example, there are many pieces titled "Kyrie," "Alleluia!" or "Praise to the Lord." Titles alone are insufficient ordering information. For best results, give as much of the following information as possible: title, composer (and arranger, if different than the composer), voice combinations (SAB, SATB, and the like), accompaniment, publisher, and publisher's number. When ordering, it helps to have a copy of the music in hand, a practice I follow when phoning an order. If for some reason you have made a mistake, or the person taking the order asks for additional information or for clarification, you can look at the cover of the piece and find everything necessary to ensure the accuracy of the order right there, e.g. "Come, Let Us Fix Our Eyes on Jesus," Kenneth T. Kosche, 2-part choir, 2 treble instruments, keyboard, CPH, 98-3198. When you order directly from the publisher, often the title and *publisher's catalog number* will be sufficient, though you may be asked to confirm the other information. Note that in the case cited, instrumental parts are also available by ordering 98-3231. Sometimes choir directors forget that instrumentalists find it easier to play from an instrumental part. In lengthier compositions, it is nearly impossible for instrumentalists to read from the choir score and turn pages while playing. Unless the instrumental parts are very expensive, I always buy at least *two sets* and keep one in the choir file. This practice has spared me more than one emergency.

It is more efficient to place an order for several selections at one time. It saves shipping expenses, and it spares the office secretary or treasurer from writing many checks in small amounts and keeping track of accounts payable. The librarian (usually me) can do the library acquisitions at one time rather than in fits and starts. Sometimes suppliers have insufficient copies of the order on hand. Then they may enter a back order; that is, they will send the quantity presently available and the balance when it becomes available. By all means, keep track of the packing slips or invoices to know when you have received everything that was ordered or to know when you have waited longer than necessary for a back order. If you phone an order, most firms will be able to tell you immediately if copies are available or if a back order will be necessary. If you feel that you cannot wait for a back order, inform the firm with which you have placed the order *immediately*, and cancel the back order. Do not wait until everything finally arrives and then return it because the order came too late. This is a poor business practice and also an unfortunate public relations move. Submit invoices promptly for payment, and keep a record of all payments, subtracting them from the available budget. It is a helpful practice to keep track of encumbered expenses—the cost of items on order for which payment has not yet been made—so that you don't exceed your budget by mistake.

Churches usually have a tax-exempt number that eliminates the payment of state sales tax. If not, you may need to ask why. Sometimes firms will assume your order to be tax-exempt because you are ordering from a church. Other times they may ask for a copy of the church's tax-exempt certificate, which should be on file. It is usually advantageous to work through only one regular dealer with whom you can establish an account and build rapport. (Years ago, after having a year off due to ill health and also having moved to a new position and location, I phoned a dealer with whom I had established a good rapport. He recognized me immediately, asked, "Where are you now?" and shipped my order that very day.) The church's business officer appreciates having fewer vendors to keep track of, as well. When ordering from them directly, some publishers give regular church customers a percentage discount. Some final, prudent advice: don't overspend the choir budget and don't spend the whole budget all at once.

Organizing the Library

Good stewardship dictates taking care of the church's assets, including the choir library. On a more selfish level for the director, it makes sense to keep the choir music organized, clean, neat, and available anytime it is needed. Some directors believe they can give away or throw out music that they don't like or plan to use. Tastes in music vary, and it may be necessary to keep an active file and an archived file due to space considerations. (The *archived* file is that big box of music next to the file cabinet left there by the previous director.) However, *all* the music in the choir library belongs to the congregation, and it is not any director's prerogative to dispose of any of the church's assets unilaterally.

Organizing the choir library involves the twin issues of storage and retrieval—keeping music in good order and finding it easily when you need it. A music library system can be as simple or as complicated as a director likes it to be. Storing music can be done in a number of ways, including the use of file cabinets, music storage boxes, and shelving. Since most choir libraries are not massive, complex cross-indexing is generally unnecessary to file and retrieve music.

I prefer to use file cabinets for choir music, if only because I have done it that way everywhere I have been for over thirty years, churches and schools alike. There are several advantages to using file cabinets. They are inexpensive and easily obtainable. Unless aesthetics are important, a used, beat-up file cabinet works as well as a new one straight from an office supply house. File cabinets can store more choir music in a smaller space than storage boxes or shelves. Music stays dust free in file cabinets. The contents of one drawer can be shifted easily to another, in case new music needs to be inserted or a change in filing system is inau-gurated.

There are some disadvantages as well. Booklets or books (Handel's *Messiah*, for instance) fare badly when stacked on edge in a file drawer, and they take up too much drawer space. Collections, chorale books, cantatas, motets, and larger works fare better stored in stacks, either on top of the file cabinets or on nearby shelves. There is a tendency to underestimate file space and try to cram too many pieces into one drawer rather than move materials from drawer to drawer. Upon occasion I have discovered that my choir librarian did this. I wonder not only how so many octavos were wedged into the drawer, but also how in the world I can extract a file for use (and dread having to put it back in the drawer). There are solutions to this problem that I will mention shortly.

Music file boxes keep music dust free and tidy. They allow a direc-tor to transport all the copies of a title handily from one location to another. There is some wasted space, however, because boxes come in fixed sizes. Sometimes the music stored in too large a box sags down in the box and conforms to that shape over time. File boxes necessitate shelves. It eventually costs more to buy storage boxes than it does to buy a cheap file cabinet to store the same quantity of music, and it takes more linear storage space for file boxes than for cabinets. However, file boxes can be rearranged easily to conform to the space available to store them. As with file drawers, booklets fare similarly in storage boxes, worse if they are allowed to sag down in too big a box.

Shelves hold stacks of music or boxes. Unless they are covered, however, shelves gather large quantities of dust. In my experience, music booklets or larger books store best when laid flat, unless they have hard covers. If necessary, lay half a dozen booklets in one direction and the next six in the opposite direction, so that the spines do not cause the pile to fall over or stack awkwardly. Stacking piles of octavos on shelves leads to either a space-use problem or a retrieval problem. If octavos are stacked only one title high, they take up a tremendous amount of space. If they are stacked one title upon another, extracting pieces from the mid-dle or bottom of a pile becomes an adventure, including trying to deter-mine where each title starts and ends in the pile. Unless piles are braced from the side, one slides into the next, and so on—a messy business.

So, that brings me back to using file cabinets for the majority of the choral library. Here is the point at which storage and retrieval are linked.

What order is best to file the music: alphabetically by title, by use (time of year, topic, etc.), by composer? My answer is "None of the above."

If music is filed alphabetically by title, room must be found to insert new titles to fit between already filed music. Then you must either leave too much dead space in each drawer contingent on possible new purchases, or you find yourself inevitably moving music from one drawer to the next each time you need to adjust for space. (Wait until four drawers in a row are completely filled, and you need to insert a new folder into the middle of the top drawer. Fun!) In addition, filing alphabetically forces one to have to remember the "something before nothing rule" (or is it "nothing before something"?—I always get this confused) or drop articles and unimportant words (do you file "A Mighty Fortress" under "A" or "Mighty"?), and things of this nature. What if you have a title in a foreign language? Do you file it under the original language or the translation? Skip the alphabetizing, thank you.

Filing by use has its attendant problems as well. Consider two titles as cases in point. Under which heading would you file "O Bride of Christ, Rejoice," Advent or Palm Sunday? The Scripture reading upon which the piece is based is appointed for both occasions in the lectionary. How about "I Know that My Redeemer Lives"? Three commonly used hymnals "file" it respectively under "Easter," "Christian Hope," and "Death and Burial." Libraries organized by seasons invariably file more than half of the music under "general use" anyway. I fail to see the advantages of this system, though there must be some since there are directors who file this way.

A well-rounded choir library contains music by many composers. Filing by composer necessitates sub-filing by arranger (alphabetically for each composer, including "anon."?), or mixing composers among arrangers in the filing organization. In my opinion, this is the least practical filing arrangement of the three suggested to this point.

My preference is to file music by voicings, number each file, and add new acquisitions to the end. Of course, some sort of accurate record either on a list, by file cards, or database is imperative, unless the choir library is miniscule and the director has a fabulous memory (something that doesn't help a *new* director one bit). I have found it convenient to use the following five categories:

SATB (mixed-voice music, including divided parts)
SAB (mixed-voice music, but not SATB)
Men's music (specifically TB, TTB, TBB, TTBB)
Women's music (specifically SA, SSA, SSAA)
Unison and two-part music (unless specifically SA or TB, including two-part mixed)

Each file bears a consecutive number and each piece of music has the corresponding file number stamped on the cover at the top or in some conspicuous place, depending upon cover art. Buy a number stamp or mark numbers by hand. Develop a coding system for the file numbers so as to not confuse SAB with SATB or women's music with unison and two-part, the most easily made filing mistake. Try something like: SATB = 1, 2, 3, etc.; SAB = 2001, 2002, 2003, etc.; Men's = 3001, 3002, 3003, etc. (By the time you have one thousand titles in each category [1999 titles under SATB] you can worry about a new numbering system.) As I file music into the drawers, I place the music *in front of* a file folder with the respective file number on it. I have not found it necessary to wrap a file folder around the music, especially when it involves fifty copies of a sixteen-page octavo. This is too bulky to fit conveniently into a single file folder. The reason for putting the folder with the file number *behind* the music is to enable anyone to see the first number in the drawer as easily as all the other numbers. At the university I number the copies in each file as well, and then assign corresponding numbers to choir folders, a practice I have never needed to do with any of my church choirs. (There are accountability reasons for me to do this at the university that I have never found necessary with the church choir.) So much for storage; now for retrieval.

Keep accurate and up-to-date records of the music files, and file music as soon as possible after use. Sloppy record keeping and stacks of unfiled music wreak havoc with a choir library. In the pre-computer era every choir director maintained several boxes of 3"x 5" library file cards. (I affectionately recall submitting a large box of annotated file cards for a graduate conducting class final project. It took me *weeks* to write them out by hand.) You may inherit a file card system at your church. If so, you must decide if you wish to continue it or convert it to a database. I keep a database for each voicing category that I print out two ways, by file number and by title. I pencil new acquisitions at the end of the list until it becomes practical to add these to the database in the computer and print out a new list. Since new acquisitions are always filed after the existing files, a director can quickly find a title purchased in the last year or two by examining the last drawer in any given category.

Some directors like to keep a single-copy file of all the music in their choir library. If you do much of your work at home, this practice may be helpful to you, but it does add an additional copy to each purchase. Also, you must then maintain two sets of files in good order. I find that keeping a database at hand is sufficient for my needs. If I require further information about specific pieces of music, I go to the choir library and pull copies for closer examination. (I *don't* need another file cabinet in my office.) However, I do find it useful to keep a small file of pieces I wish to examine further to consider for purchase. Once these titles are added to the choir library, there is no need for me to keep personal copies, generally speaking.

Over time and with frequent use, the library holdings become very familiar to a director. Sometimes it is possible to put your hands on a file without having to consult the records. This is a good kind of familiarity to have developed. If several people need to have access to the choir library, be careful to suggest to them that they all agree to follow the same filing system, treating the church's assets with proper care.

Chapter 8
Musical Growth

At some time or another every church choir director fills many subsidiary roles: music librarian, business manager, recruitment officer, publicity director, director of personnel, sales representative, stagehand, custodian. There are days when it seems as if far more of your time and effort is consumed in activities related to one of the job titles just listed than in musical activities. Even a part-time volunteer church choir director cannot completely escape most of these duties. However, one of the most natural and important roles not yet enumerated is that of teacher. This chapter is concerned with a few facets of musical growth affecting choir members and directors alike.

Teaching the Choir

Many fine choir directors are good teachers at heart, whether they have formal educational preparation in curriculum, methods, and materials or not. Even an inexperienced choir director needs to create opportunities that will afford musical growth for the choir. Most choir members need to sight-read better and to improve their vocal technique, as well. The effectiveness of a choir is directly related to the individual abilities of its members to read and interpret musical scores well and to produce a beautiful and expressive singing tone. Directors ought to be able to assist their members to grow in both of these areas. Although there are many times throughout a rehearsal when the director can teach the choir, the warm-up period provides a prime opportunity to address these areas, while it simultaneously prepares the choir for the main work of the rehearsal.

Using Warm-ups Effectively

What kinds of warm-ups are there? How can they be used effectively in a rehearsal? The answer to the first question is somewhat akin to the fellow who ordered a 12" pizza and said, "Cut the pizza in six pieces instead of eight. I'm not so hungry tonight." I'm going to cut the warm-up pie into *four* big pieces: spiritual, physical, vocal, and technical warm-ups. A director can doubtlessly foster growth generally through the use of any of these, and *musical* growth specifically by means of the final two. The effectiveness question has a two-part answer. Part one lies in the design of warm-ups and the application to actual repertoire the choir is singing. Second, no matter how well-conceived a warm-up may be, its effectiveness is diminished if the choir members do not participate with full attention. Some singers merely go through the motions of warm-ups without thoroughly engaging their minds in the process. A director can unwittingly foster inattention by using the same warm-ups rehearsal after rehearsal. Mindless routine kills the effectiveness of otherwise valid exercises. Therefore, the effectiveness issue finds its answer in how directly the warm-up relates to the needs of the choir and how intently the members participate.

"Spiritual warm-ups" are the kinds that give incentives to the choir to sing: present perspectives about the music to be sung and focus thoughts by means of a Scripture reading, devotion, or prayer. For the choir that meets in the morning, it helps to start the day by first concentrating on spiritual matters before becoming consumed with the cares of the day. At an evening rehearsal it is comforting to set the bruises of the day's battles aside by commending them to the Lord and prepare joyfully to sing God's praises. Indeed, the writer of Psalm 92 recommends this course of action to us. It isn't necessary for all the Scripture readings, devotions, and prayers to concern only musical matters. Over the years, I have experienced many thoughtful devotions presented by choir members that brought the choir together as a concerned community over personal, parish, or national matters. A prayer or devotion centers the *spirits* of the singers as it focuses their thoughts on the common task ahead.

Physical warm-ups prepare *minds* and *bodies* for singing. In some cases, it is necessary to get everyone's blood flowing and invigorate them mentally and physically. In other cases, it is more advantageous to use warm-ups to soothe weary minds and bodies through stretching, bending, or shoulder-rubbing exercises that release tension. A director needs to tailor the choice of the warm-ups and the energy level required to do them to the needs of the choir. I have used vigorous rhythmic speech and action warm-ups to awaken lethargic singers, and simple stretching and shoulder rolling movements to work out built-up stresses. I advocate a short physical warm-up at the beginning of every rehearsal, even for the brief Sunday morning warm-up when there may only be time to stretch. Sometimes I give my choir a simple suggestion such as, "Stretch out to warm-up," and then I let the singers select for themselves what they wish to do from among the several stretching exercises in our repertoire. In fact, many times I find singers doing some stretching and wiggling movements on their own before the rehearsal officially begins. These choir members may be creatures of habit, but they also realize direct personal benefits from physical warm-ups, or they wouldn't take the initiative to do them ahead of time.

You may occasionally find it helpful to pause in mid-rehearsal and quickly change the physical positions of your singers or have them do a very brief physical motion to break the established set. The easiest way to do this is to have the choir stand if sitting or sit if standing. When possible avoid prolonged periods of either sitting or standing through a rehearsal. Prolonged sitting actually fosters mental and physical fatigue. "The mind can only absorb as much as the rear end can sit," as the saying goes.

You can easily develop a large repertoire of physical warm-ups of your own, but here is a short list to get you thinking. I am purposely leaving breathing exercises to the "vocal warm-ups" category, though breathing exercises clearly involve physical activity. All of the activities in *Figure 19* should be done while standing.

Figure 19: Physical Warm-ups

Roll shoulders forward and backward. (Try moving both shoulders simultaneously in opposite directions!)
With feet positioned directly under the hips, stretch tall from the top of the head.
Lift both arms and reach tall, keeping feet on ground.
Standing tall, press the heels of both hands downward at each side.
Do this with arms extended in front of the body. (Also with hands upraised.)
Walk in place but do not lift toes from the ground.
With feet planted directly under hips (not a wide spread), twist the torso from side to side.
Do a "rag doll" by drooping forward at the waist.
Slowly raise the body again to an upright position. (Do this to a specific count.)
"Scrunch" shoulders up, hold, and release. (Do this several times rapidly.)
Shake out arms, focusing on keeping loose wrists and fingers.
Turn sideways in each row and gently massage the shoulders of the person who is standing next to you.

Note that from time to time a choir member might express a disinclination to do one of these activities. Whenever this occurs in my rehearsals, I never make an issue of it. The reason for the disinclination is usually apparent to me, e.g. illness, injury. I use the shoulder-rubbing

activity sparingly because in any group at least one person feels uncom-
fortable doing this. I believe it is important to respect a person's right to
his or her personal space. If any particular physical activity annoys or
distresses the choir, don't use it. You can accomplish your goals by sub-
stituting a different activity for one that is out of favor at the moment. As
I have already stated, physical warm-ups miss their full potential if
singers let their minds wander and do not fully engage in the activity.

If I am pressed for time, or if I haven't centered my own mind on a
specific routine for the beginning of a rehearsal, and consequently
neglecting to engage the choir in either a spiritual or physical warm-up,
the rehearsal invariably doesn't feel quite "right." Also, someone in the
choir is absolutely certain to remind me, "You forgot the prayer! We
didn't stretch!"—or some similar comment. There are times when we
begin a rehearsal with something physical followed by a prayer or devotional thought, and there are other times the order is reversed.

Helen Kemp has developed a wonderful little chant, which goes like
this: "Body, mind, spirit, voice—it takes *the whole person* to sing and
rejoice!" She is entirely correct. So far we have dealt briefly with body,
mind, and spirit. Now, we move on to the voice.

Breathing exercises are physical activities as well as vocal techniques.
For the sake of this discussion, I prefer to attach breathing warm-ups to
vocal techniques. Here is the reason, and in a way, it harkens back to the
discussion on giving pitches to the choir. The singing process begins
with a mental concept, is powered by the breath, finds sound in the vocal
folds, is shaped by the parts of the mouth, and is finally projected by the
head and body. If you like, you can remember the following five-part
"–tion" list to summarize the singing process: initiation, actuation, phona-
tion, articulation, and resonation. A weakness in any part of this chain of
events is a fault in vocal technique. (Some faults are more fatal than others, needless to say.)

Building Vocal Technique

There is a measure of difficulty for a choral director to give what
appears to be a massed voice lesson to a choir. First, to be completely
dedicated to each individual singer's needs, one-on-one time is essential.
Second, a director may observe most people in the choir producing the
desired technique, and say "Good!" This may inadvertently reinforce an

incorrect technique in a few singers. The director is constantly challenged to communicate simultaneously to a wide variety of singers with different vocal backgrounds, fortifying good habits, and reforming bad ones. Third, there is a finite period of rehearsal time available to a church choir for building vocal techniques, so the effect must be viewed as cumulative, though occasionally a gross fault can be corrected quickly, or at least minimized. Before we get more deeply into this topic than might be appropriate to a "novice's guide," let me limit the warm-ups presented under "Voice Building" to some basic breathing exercises and vocalises. Check the resources section for books and video presentations that explore this area in more detail.

Your choir members will have heard a plethora of singing styles when visiting other churches, in concerts, radio broadcasts, audio tapes, and compact discs. Which single sound is "correct?" Although good vocal technique rests on a body of physiological evidence in addition to aesthetic values, singing is an art, not a "science." If a singer claims artistic license to make any sort of squawk he or she feels appropriate, you cannot call the resulting sound "wrong." You can, however, disclaim its appropriateness to your choral setting and point the singer to some commonly accepted norms for breathing, vocalizing, and shaping language.

Nothing affects a singer's sound as directly as the breath the singer takes in anticipation of vocalizing. A relaxed, free breath enables a relaxed, free sound. A short, quick, tense breath produces a correspondingly tense or thin sound. It is not difficult to demonstrate this, and in fact, by having the singers take a breath inappropriately and asking them to sing, they may hear and feel the difference more vividly than if you describe it to them. As a didactic device, whether related to breathing or some other technique, have your singers exaggerate an incorrect technique, to which you immediately reply, "Now, *DON'T DO* that again, *ever!*" After the invariable good laugh together that follows, you can show them a better technique. Making a comparison immediately is essential. By the way, a good belly laugh is a great breathing exercise! *Figure 20* lists just a few of many possible warm-up exercises for developing a better breathing technique with your singers. You can probably adapt many of these in a creative way to your own singers.

Figure 20: Breathing Warm-ups

Standing tall, but relaxed, blow out the residual air in the lungs through the
mouth
(start by blowing out air, not breathing in—create the need to breathe).
Relax and let the air fill the lungs to a resting (quiet respiration) level.
Repeat this exercise several times, noting that the rib cage is held high, the
singers' shoulders do not droop on exhaling, and their heads remain in
a tall vertical alignment.
Repeat the exercise, but each time fill the lungs to an ever-increasing capacity,
noting the singers' shoulders do not rise with inhalation or droop with
exhalation.
Breathe out and when the singers think they are out of breath have them count
to 4 out loud, ensuring deeper exhalation and creating more need for
breath
(increase the length of the counting from four to eight).
Exhale with a hissing sound (friction caused by tongue and teeth only), and
then blow the rest of the air out and inhale.
Puppy pant but do so without making the noise caused by a restricted throat or
high tongue
(I am constantly amazed at how many people find this difficult to do).
Breathe out and do a "rag doll;" then breathe in slowly while standing tall.
Have the singers hold a hand in a "thumbs up" position at arm's length in front
of them and ask them to quickly "blow the candle out" (must be done
in a burst of air, not slowly).
Have the singers inhale very quickly as if suddenly surprised. Then imitate this
abdominal action with a more sustained breath.
After a breath out, a deep breath in, have the singers vocalize on a comfortable
unison pitch (later a chord) on any vowel of choice, starting with the
most open, "Ah." Precede the vowel (on the exact same pitch – no
scooping or sliding) with a consonant sound to avoid the glottal attack
so many will use. Select from the following: th, v, z, f, l, m, n.

Of course, breathing exercises without making music become dull
after a while, or the singers may disconnect the exercise from actual
singing. Then the warm-ups may become virtually useless, detracting
from the process of skill building. *Figure 20* is arranged in a somewhat
sequential pedagogical order. After a few weeks of doing the first several, move on to the next one or two, only touching on the first. I have
often found that a slightly extended period of breathing warm-ups helps
to reinvigorate choir members when everyone is very tired. It goes without saying that the air they have to breathe must be fresh and full of oxy-
gen. (Oh, great! Your choir room is in the basement of the church with
no ventilation—see the paragraph in chapter one about having a member
of the trustees/property management board in the choir.)

Let's connect breathing warm-ups to vocalizing warm-ups. *Figure 21* shows some common vocalizing configurations. The more extensive ones obviously do not permit many repetitions at successive pitch levels. *Figure 22* gives piano chord progressions you can play to accompany several vocal configurations consecutively by ascending chromatically. The top pitch of the white note chord is the same as that of the black note transition chord but written *enharmonically* (meaning in essence that C sharp sounds the same as D flat, D sharp sounds the same as E flat, and so on). Unfortunately, there is no smooth way to play chord progressions that descend chromatically. Anything I have ever tried sounds musically awkward, except simply playing the first chord of the new key. *Figure 23* is one of my favorites for gradually expanding vocal range and projection. When vocalizing the entire choir, it is important to remember that some singers have wider ranges than others; so it is a good thing to provide them the opportunity to use and even stretch their ranges while safeguarding the voices of those with more limited ranges. When I use these vocalises, I am always careful to say, "Stop when you cannot comfortably continue." Or, I make the analogy to doing physical exercises by saying, "If you can do five sit-ups, you will never be able to do six unless you try, but you should not expect to go from five to twenty-five all at once!"

Figure 21: Thirds, Fifths, and Octaves

Figure 22: Accompanying Chromatic Chord Progressions

Figure 23: Rising Sixth Exercise

etc.

Singers may effectively use various combinations of vowels and consonants with all of these exercises. Consider the beginning "Y" of "yah"
to be in actuality an "E" sung quickly. The "E" sound should occur, as
all the consonants should, just *before* the beat on which the vowel is to
begin. This is a general rule of good singing: vowels sound ON the beat;
beginning consonants sound BEFORE the beat. If your choir has difficulty with this, have them sing a musical passage using only vowels.
This may sound a little silly to them at first, but if you and they are
patient, they can learn to put the vowels ON the beat and simultaneously
sing with a nice, smooth *legato* sound. Then have them lightly and
crisply insert consonants before the beat. (Have a little fun with the choir
and ask them to sing only the consonants. I think you will establish the
point that beautiful singing is primarily the work of the vowels.)

Developing Tonal Sensitivity

Many church choirs rely heavily on an accompanying instrument,
usually piano or organ. If you listen carefully to choirs that have such

95

reliance, you may hear the choir singing ever so slightly after the piano or organ plays. This means the singers have developed very good listening reflexes in order to match the keyboard. They have become expert "followers." You may experience the same phenomenon with an individual who demurs to sing alone but will sing *with* someone else. There are several ways to eliminate this habit in the choir, putting the vowels on the beat and the consonants before the beat being one of them. The biggest reason many singers "follow" the accompaniment is their own insecurity with the music. Of course, practicing a piece until it is very well known is another solution, but you can also assist the choir to have a more confident grasp of each piece if they have developed a sense of tonality. Much of the music sung in church choirs is logical from a tonal standpoint. Melodies and harmonies, while not totally predictable (wouldn't *that* be boring?) don't occur as random events. They exist with a certain logic called tonality. I believe having a good sense of tonality is a necessary precursor to good sight reading, a topic we shall take up in a moment.

Most music, probably all music, your choir will sing is *tonal*, that is, it has a key feeling such as D major or E-minor, and the like. Even though a longer piece may progress through a number of related keys, the music has a tonal center rather than seeming like pitches selected by chance (a simplistic definition of *atonality*). The term *tonality* implies that different tones have different musical functions. The home tone or the name for the family we call D major is "D," for example. "F" is the home tone, called the *tonic*, of the key of "F," and so on. In every key there are several other significant pitch functions that define a key to our ears. The next most important pitches to the tonic are the dominant (the fifth tone of a key) and the subdominant (the fourth tone). For those who read music well, their eye defines key areas also; that is, a person who understands what we term music theory can recognize tonal functions. A singer who couples aural experience (some people call this "ear training") with so-called music theory experience becomes a better sight-reader as a consequence. This is not a mystery. Too many singers do not make sound-to-symbol connections. Too many music theory students think of that course of study as some sort of higher mathematics and not *musicianship*, but that is another story. To my mind music "theory" is an unfortunate term.

It is wishful thinking to imagine that everyone in a church choir cares to know about music theory. A director can waste much valuable rehearsal time trying too hard to convert them. However, all singers can easily gain a sense of tonal memory approached in a systematic way. Notice that every pattern in *Figure 21* begins and ends with the tonic. Even singers with a "tin ear" can determine that. It doesn't hurt to point out the tonic, by the way. The pattern that rises a fifth goes from *tonic* to *dominant* (I – V). Point this out to the choir, too.

Figure 24: Chord Progression in Close Position

Figure 25: Chord Progression in Open Positions

I use a simple set of chord progressions that the choir can easily sing to get a sense of tonality in their ears. In *Figures 24* and *25* a very basic chord progression is given first in "close position," the parts are as close as they can be in pitch, and then in successively more "open positions." (As one chord changes to another chord, we say it *progresses*, hence, the term *chord progression*.)

Notice that I have tied pitches from chord to chord that are common to each. Look closely and you can see that there are only four different melodic patterns used at various times in the voice parts. The basses can easily memorize their part, but the other voices have three melodies to memorize. Note also that the bass part always sings the same part, what we term the *root* of the chord. Have the choir sing these parts on a variety of vowel sounds with a variety of consonant beginnings, just as you did for the patterns in *Figures 21* and *23*. It is important to take vocal ranges into consideration when you give starting pitches so that one part is not pushed into an extreme range while the others may still be singing in a comfortable zone. Of course, one can devise more complicated progressions, as one desires, but having the sound of this basic chord progression indelibly in the memory of the singers will pay dividends to the choir in terms of better intonation and more accurate singing generally. In fact, when you have the choir sing the progression, insist on good intonation. Have them stop as chords change and adjust tuning by individuals or sections as needed. The more you do this at first, the less you need to do so later. Singers will subconsciously trust their instincts in simpler music to know where chord progressions are likely to lead, based on their experience with this basic progression. A director can conduct *crescendi* and *decrescendi* while the choir sings this common progression, ask for rhythmic singing (repeated staccato notes for each pitch), and all sorts of other musical ideas can be incorporated to make the experience interesting, adding a new musical dimension as the choir gains skill in developing tonal memory.

Improving Sight Reading

The more readily the singers read music, the easier the choir learns new pieces. As a consequence, the choir is enabled to sing with a greater subtlety of expression. There is nothing deadlier from rehearsal to rehearsal than to find a choir and director pounding notes as if music making were only a drill to be endured. Though it is often necessary to work sections of music in detail, nobody really draws deep satisfaction from the repetition necessary to learn all parts by rote. I mentioned before that many singers fail to make a connection between sound and symbol. It is the director's responsibility to enhance every opportunity for the singers to establish these kinds of connections. If you reflect for a moment, in simplified terms, music is composed of sounds that are longer or shorter (*duration*), higher or lower (*pitch*), and louder or softer (*dynamics*) than one another, and, as previously stated, relate to one another in rhythmic groups (*meter*) and around a home tone or tonic (*tonality*). Of course, that is a very simple way to describe the essence of music, but singers who can relate these basic concepts to the way they are described when written (*music notation*) find themselves reading music. Sight-reading describes the process by which a person looks at an unfamiliar piece of music and is able to sing the music accurately at a certain level of proficiency without first resorting to hearing it sung by someone else and then memorizing what is heard (*rote* learning).

There are some good materials available to guide a choir to better reading ability, but the average church choir may not have the time to invest in a curricular program in sight-reading. Without resorting to a textbook course, a director can enhance the ability of his or her singers to read music. In keeping with the spirit of a guide for novices, I won't be very detailed, but rather will sketch some ideas for the creative director to explore more deeply. These ideas concern tonality, pitch, and rhythm reading.

I cannot stress highly enough the value of orienting singers to a sense of key or tonality. The nice feature about tonality is that major sounds like major, irrespective of which pitch is tonic. The same is true for minor and modal tonalities. By using the exercise in *Figure 24* and lowering the tenor first pitch one half-step in the first chord and the alto pitch one half-step in the second, you can change the exercise from major to minor. Then note the corresponding pitches in *Figure 25* for open position chords and do the same thing there. By this means, the so-called "building blocks" or principal chord movements in major and minor tonality can be established in singers' ears and minds without their having to look at a written score. It is helpful to have all singers learn all parts of this exercise, although when it is sung, the basses need to sing the bass part only. In fact, it is the bass part that establishes the tonality. Theoretically, the bass section should be among your best sight readers for this reason. (Theory and reality sometimes diverge in this respect.) Take opportunities to point out musical movement that reminds the singers of these exercises when you come across similar harmonies in pieces they are singing. Furthermore, have all members of the choir sing portions of the bass part from time to time, particularly when the bass part functions as a true bass part and not purely melodically. This experience will sensitize the choir further to functional tonality. Some hymnals are written in a rather conservative style with chordal harmony throughout. Even hymnals that have more adventuresome harmonies designed for keyboard players contain many hymns that are singable in parts. Reading these hymns from time to time assists in sight-reading. Of course, the sopranos need to sing another part than the melody. Flip-flop the tenor and bass, soprano and alto, when you can do so. Have all parts sing the tenor, for example, while you accompany the hymn at the piano.

Pitch reading is not as difficult as it appears to some of the singers. Some express trepidation about reading the bass clef. I suppose one can use the "every good boy does fine" routine for the lines in the treble clef, and "all cows eat grass" for the spaces in the bass clef as a starter. However, the singers must quickly recognize pitch names without having to run through the mnemonic each time. For fun, remind them of what would likely happen if they first had to figure out what S-T-O-P meant while driving before they took action. For those who fear the bass clef (often sopranos or altos) having them frequently sing with the tenors and basses will in short time alleviate their anxieties. Knowing pitch names is less important than *understanding pitch functions.* When reading a new part, relate the sound of certain important pitches in the part to their positions on a staff. When the same pitch appears, it must sound the same as well. In this way, singers begin to approximate high, low, and same, or skip, step, same without worrying first about nomenclature. Get the sound in their ears first; give sounds a name later.

Some singers insist on sight-reading by melodic intervals, e.g. major third, perfect fourth, minor sixth, and the like. There is benefit to this procedure but also a pitfall. If a singer starts on the wrong pitch, the whole phrase can end up wrong, something that happened in a perform-ance I directed many years ago, and the experience lodged itself in my memory. Even if some intervals are sung incorrectly, singers can return to the home key at phrase endings or *cadences* if they think tonally rather than by intervals. Tonal function, therefore, gives context to intervallic accuracy. It is more important to approach sight-reading from a tonal, harmonic perspective than from the intervallic relationship of individual pitches. *Combining* a sense of tonality with concepts of intervals is the ultimate in developing sight-reading skills.

Reading rhythm is the downfall of many singers. Probably because of the lessons needed to master instruments, players tend to have a well-developed sense of rhythm. Many singers are blissfully unaware of the fact that some pitches are longer than others, that they have a relationship to the beat, or that they are organized in groups called meter. Some have developed the misguided notion that the quarter note always gets the beat. Consequently, music written in 3/2, or some pieces in 4/4, in which the pulse is actually the half note, confuses them. The pulse in much 6/8

100

music is the dotted quarter, not the eighth note. A useful device for developing rhythmic accuracy with a choir is tapping or clapping the beat against individual parts. Have one section lightly tap the beat while another section lightly claps the rhythm of its own part. Be careful to use a style of clapping that is light and crisp, fingers across fingers, for example, and not resembling applause. In order to relate pitch to rhythm, singers can both clap and sing at the same time (like walking and chewing gum). It has been frequently said that instrumentalists would gain melodic grace by singing their parts more frequently, and singers would gain a better rhythmic sense by playing their parts. I think this is good advice. Having the choir speak parts rhythmically allows the choir to focus on rhythm without concern for pitch accuracy. If you have your choir speak rhythms, try to have them keep a live sound during sustained or longer notes.

It seems to me, once again, that accurately naming rhythms is less important at first than experiencing rhythmic patterns. After the experience in rhythmic sound, give the symbols for the rhythm names. Since there are fewer rhythmic symbols than pitch names, learning to recognize whole notes, half notes, and the like should be easier than learning the pitch names on both staves. Singers need to know that pitch and rhythm cooperate in music but exist independently of one another. This is also true of dynamics. Some young children equate "high" with "fast" and "loud," and they equate "low" with "slow" and "soft." A director can teach young singers to differentiate among these concepts.

Working with Problem Voices

Speaking of differentiating among concepts, one must be careful not to equate a so-called "problem voice" with a "difficult personality." I define problem voices as belonging to singers who seemingly cannot control the sounds they sing to blend well, match pitches well, or transition registers well (singing in the wrong octave, for example). A volunteer choir may contain one or more of these voices. Unless you wish to eliminate the singers with vocal problems by means of an audition, you should be prepared to offer some assistance to them to help them improve their singing skills. Here are a few ideas.

Blend is best achieved when vocal timbre and dynamics are under control. Some singers have learned odd concepts of vowel formation. In other cases, regional pronunciation differences are set into stark con-

101

trast when the choir contains members from various parts of the country. Uniformity of vowels can be conveniently taught when singing some of the exercises suggested in *Figures 21* through *24*. When a vowel sound "jumps" out of the musical texture of a particular phrase, it is best to model the desired sound and practice it with the entire choir in the context of the piece. A director needs patience to shape the sounds the way he or she wants. Speech patterns take years to develop, and they cannot be completely changed overnight, even if the singer is determined to make appropriate adaptations. (I remember as a first year high school choral director being asked, "Why are you criticizing the way we speak?" in reference to my attempt to coax a nice round "oo" for the middle of a central Illinoisan "Alleluia.")

If individual singers sing too loudly in a group, balance as well as blend is affected. Sometimes loud singing is a result of a hearing loss, causing the singer not to have a realistic appraisal of his or her own voice. A baritone in one of my first choirs seemed also to have a brash and outspoken personality. This trait and his inability to blend annoyed some of the choir members. It turned out that all of this was caused by a hearing loss. The problem subsided after he acquired a hearing aid. Some singers simply get wrapped up in their singing, and in their fervor do not realize they are causing a blend problem. It is the duty of the director gently to correct the sound levels to an appropriate level by conducting gestures or by speaking with the individual privately.

Matching pitches, singing with the proper vocal registration, or singing in the wrong octave (usually men sing too low) presents the greatest challenge. Some singers have never re-mastered control of their voices after their teenage "mutant" years. This is especially true of men, although I have encountered a few women who manifest these difficulties. A director cannot take the time in a rehearsal to correct a chronic problem singer with register problems. In fact, doing so can be embarrassing to the singer. However, ignoring the problem or hoping it will go away on its own is not an adequate solution. Perhaps the singer and director can meet at times other than the choir rehearsal for a little vocal coaching. I have encountered a half dozen or so voices like this over the years and have felt the need to spend some private time with each singer. In each case, I discovered the singer had no clear notion of the sound being sung in comparison to the sound that was required. It was first necessary to establish the singer's actual practical range, usually restricted and low, and then work with the singer to enable him or her to match pitches successfully *and to know when success had been achieved.* It is not enough for singers to match a given pitch. It is essential that singers evaluate when they have done so accurately and take corrective action when they have not. I have usually found greater success in my *singing* the pitches to be matched rather than playing them on the piano. This is my general process: first I sing a pitch, then ask for the choir member to sing it back to me, and finally ask, "Did you sing the *same* pitch as I, or did you sing *higher* or *lower*?" Moving around a small vocal range, we do this until the person generally responds correctly, both as to answering correctly and as to matching the pitches more accurately. My next question is, *"How much* higher/lower did you sing?" At this point I accept answers such as "a little higher," or "quite a bit lower." Gradually a singer begins to self-evaluate more accurately, understanding the breath level and energy necessary to sing accurately over a wider pitch range. Higher pitches need to be sung in a lighter registration. Otherwise, a singer gets the notion that is it necessary to shout to sing above a certain pitch. Consult a good vocal pedagogy book or a competent voice teacher for more details.

Growing as a Director

Simply being on the job for a few years will result in some growth as a director. For those who have degrees in music, there are uncountable matters to be learned that cannot be adequately taught in classes. For a novice with little academic musical background or vocal pedagogy, the process of growth can appear daunting, though exciting. I have found that individuals in the field for years, including, perhaps *especially*, those who have degrees and many years of experience, are generous in sharing counsel and advice. Of course, a music degree program is an established way to learn more about the field, but it may not be a viable option. Many organizations exist for the mutual support and edification of their memberships. These organizations hold workshops, conferences, publish periodicals, and recommend literature to these ends. Novices need not feel shy or embarrassed to join one or more professional musical organizations. Larger metropolitan areas often have a "guild" established by local parish musicians for their mutual support. You may be genuinely surprised how many directors have similar musical needs and trepidations to your own, though some people would not come up directly to you to admit the fact. Perhaps you can start a loose confederation of directors in your denomination or across denominational lines in your area to share information and discover new ideas together. It is difficult to grow as a director if you feel isolated. My best advice is to get connected to others in the profession as soon as possible, even if because of your geographic location or personal circumstances your connection is as tenuous as merely reading the monthly journal published by most organizations. You will find some references in the resources section.

Approaching New Music

Some choirs sing the same repertoire year after year as if nothing else of quality exists or matters. Perhaps this notion has developed because of leadership too afraid to try something different or unacquainted with how to find new music. Whatever the reason, there is no excuse for running the choir into a rut or refusing to get them out of one of their own making. One of my publisher friends likes to say, "If I don't know the piece, it's new to me!" To this I may add a Lutheran "This is most certainly true!" It was once possible to speak of the "standard choral repertoire" for church choirs, but I believe this is no longer true, if indeed it ever was completely true. For a novice director, there may be some quality music lurking in the files that has not been sung for years; hence, it would be new to almost everyone. On the other hand, publishers continue to bring out reams of literature every year, though one must not accept uncritically that every recently published octavo is of equal quality with every other. Tastes vary, as does musical quality. It is necessary to use discernment when selecting new repertoire.

When I look for new music for my choirs, I search for compositions or arrangements in which the text and music are fit for each other. The text must be of a high quality, must convey a message worth conveying in phrases using language skillfully and occasionally memorably. There are so many trite texts set to music. *Trite texts* are suitable for *trite religion*.

The tune set to the text ought to reflect the word accents appropriately, i.e., all the syllables should have proper weight as to accent and importance of meaning. The musical style must match the character of the text, as well. A tall order? Yes, indeed! If more directors were fussier about the music they purchased, the quality of published music would improve tremendously and banality would disappear. A colleague once ruefully observed, "We must through much *trivialization* enter the Kingdom of God." Another observed, "Simple music need not be simple-minded." You have the duty as choir director to set the musical and textual standard for your choir. Take the time to be critical, providing your choir and congregation with quality texts matched by well-crafted music.

The musical organizations referenced in the previous section often publish reviews of newly released music or provide reading sessions at their gatherings. Publisher showcases abound. Not to be overlooked is the vast resource available over the World Wide Web. Because web sites change, it is not profitable for me to list current addresses here. However, you can locate home pages of most major publishers on the web by using the following formula: www.*publisher*.com (or *.org*).

Some locales have large music retail outlets to which you can go to browse through choral music at your convenience. If your church or school has an established account with one of these stores, permission may be given to take a stack of single copies home "on approval" to look over in your home or office. I do this periodically by a sort of triage process. There are some pieces in the music bins that look immediately appealing, some which may have appeal upon further review, and some that I have no interest in at all. I have learned that the categories I just mentioned are miniscule, small, and huge, respectively. You may need to look through a hundred octavos to find two or three eminently suitable to your choir's needs. Do not let this come to you as a shock. Over time you will recognize publishers and composers who seem to provide you with a higher quantity of suitable materials. Naturally, your attention may be drawn to them more readily. Learn not to dwell on pieces that have little immediate appeal to you, for whatever reason, unless you have a tremendous amount of free time.

Expanding Musical Horizons

From time to time, try singing some music with your choir that pushes the boundaries of your and their experience. This may mean trying to sing music with an interesting vocal combination, one that uses instruments with the choir, one that uses unusual instrumental combinations, or perhaps one with an intriguing text. Unless the reaction from the choir or the parish as a whole is vehemently negative, you may need to persevere through a little inevitable resistance to something new and different. Of course, you will have to gauge when you are expanding musical horizons for yourself and the choir, or whether you have "pushed the envelope too far," in contemporary parlance. Occasionally, you will find a gem of a piece that at first glance seems highly unusual but suddenly fits a context for the parish. This is an area for which the experience of others can have great benefit for you. Go to hear other good choirs in your town and support touring groups. Many college and university choirs travel all over the country, presenting a variety of repertoire and musical styles. It may be desirable to build a small library of quality choral recordings to which you may refer for ideas or which you may play for your church choir as examples of good choral singing.

In short, if it excites you to do so, there are many ways to continue to grow in personal knowledge, understanding, and appreciation of the great art of choral music. When you do so, you have the privilege of leading others into a deeper appreciation, as well. That *is* exciting!

Concluding Thoughts

I hope you will find many ideas in this book to be useful to you in fulfilling more efficiently and effectively the multifaceted duties of a church choir director. I've tried to blend the discussion throughout into a mix of principles and practice from my perspective that I felt to be important. Furthermore, I hope you will be so engaged in the activity that you will want to explore some of the issues presented in these pages in greater detail. For this reason, I have included a few references to assist you. While one may always take satisfaction from a job well done when director and choir together use their musical gifts to the best of their abilities, neither singers nor director should become complacent. There is always room for growth. As director, you are in a unique position to initiate growth for yourself and for your choir.

In the preceding pages I have recorded some of my thoughts about leading church choirs, borne of years of experience working with many fine Christian people. When I first started directing, I was high in energy and short on skill. After these many years, I have less energy, but I think my experience enables me to manage my resources better. My choirs have taught me well. I am deeply indebted to them for their many hours of hard work and perseverance, love and patience, faith and devotion—and forgiveness. Without dedicated and understanding choristers, directors can accomplish little. I speak from experience.

Novice and experienced directors alike enjoy a high privilege to serve with their choirs in the task of ennobling public worship and proclaiming the Gospel through song. Doing so is both a solemn obligation and a sacred joy. May God bless you and your singers with great joy as you work together in musical ministry.

Resources

Organizations

Denominational

Association of Anglican Musicians (AAM)
Communications Office
28 Ashton Road
Fort Mitchell, KY 41017
859.344.9308 phone and fax
AnglicanM@aol.com
www.anglicanmusicians.org

Association of Lutheran Church Musicians (ALCM)
P.O. Box 6064
Ellicott City, MD 21042
800.624.2526
410.480.2490 fax
ALCM@valpo.edu
www.alcm.org

Fellowship of American Baptist Musicians (FABM)
1600 Tall Tree Drive
Trenton, MI 48183
313.277.7995
313.277.2167 fax
PJPMWWW@aol.com
www.fabm.com

**Fellowship of United Methodists in Music and Worship Arts
(FUMMWA)**
P.O. Box 24787
Nashville, TN 37202
800.952.8977
615.749.6874 fax
FUMMWA@aol.com
www.fummwa.org

National Association of Pastoral Musicians (NPM)
225 Sheridan Street NW
Washington, D.C. 20011-1452
202.723.5800
202.723.2262 fax
NPMSING@npm.org
www.npm.org

Presbyterian Association of Musicians (PAM)
100 Witherspoon Street
Louisville, KY 40202-1396
888.728.7228
502.569.8465 fax
www.horeb.pcusa.org/pam

Southern Baptist Church Music Conference (SBCMC)
Carson Newman College
Box 71934
Jefferson City, TN 37760
www.sbcmc.org

Professional/Non-denominational

American Choral Directors Association (ACDA)
502 SW 38th Street
Lawton, OK 73505
580.355.8161
580.248.1465
ACDA@ACDAonline.org
www.acdaonline.org

American Guild of English Handbell Ringers (AGEHR)
1055 East Centerville Station Road
Dayton, OH 45459
800.878.5459
937.438.0085 fax
executive@agehr.org
www.agehr.org

American Guild of Organists (AGO)
475 Riverside Drive, Suite 1260
New York, NY 10115
212.870-2310
212.870.2163 fax
info@agohq.org
www.agohq.org

Choristers Guild
2834 West Kingsley Road
Garland, TX 75041
972.271.1521
972.840.3113
choristers@choristersguild.org
www.choristersguild.org

The Hymn Society in the United States and Canada
745 Commonwealth Avenue
Boston, MA
800.THE.HYMN
617.353.7322 fax
hymnsoc@bu.edu
www.bu.edu/sth/hymn

Books

Children's/Youth Choirs

Edwards, Randy. *Revealing Riches and Building Lives*. St. Louis:
MorningStar, 2000.

Kemp, Helen. *Of Primary Importance, Vol. 1*. Garland, TX: Choristers
Guild.

Kemp, Helen. *Of Primary Importance*, *Vol. 2*. Garland, TX: Choristers
Guild.

McRae, Shirley W. *Directing the Children's Choir: a Comprehensive
Resource*. New York: Schirmer Books, 1990.

Rotermund, Donald, ed. *Children Sing His Praise*. St. Louis: Concordia, 1985.

Stultz, Marie. *Innocent Sounds*. St. Louis: MorningStar, 1999.

Yarrington, John. *Building the Youth Choir*. Minneapolis: Augsburg Fortress, 1990.

Church Music History

Wilson-Dickson, Andrew. *The Story of Christian Music*. Minneapolis: Augsburg Fortress, 1996.

Conducting/Choral Techniques

Bertalot, John. *Immediately Practical Tips for Choral Directors*. Minneapolis: Augsburg Fortress, 1994.

Decker, Harold A., and Colleen J. Kirk. *Choral Conducting: Focus on Communication*. Englewood Cliffs, NJ: Prentice-Hall, 1988.

Decker, Harold A., and Julius Herford (eds.). *Choral Conducting: a Symposium*. Englewood Cliffs, NJ: Prentice-Hall, 1973.

Ehmann, Wilhelm. *Choral Directing*. Minneapolis: Augsburg Fortress, 2001. [paperback ed.].

Green, Elizabeth. *The Modern Conductor*, 6th ed. Englewood Cliffs, NJ: Prentice-Hall, 1997.

Jennings, Kenneth. *Sing Legato*. San Diego, CA: Kjos. V74 choir book; V74A accomp. book

McElheran, Brock. *Conducting Technique*, rvsd. ed. New York: Oxford University Press, 1989.

Meek, Charles J. *Conducting Made Easy for Directors of Amateur Musical Organizations*. Metuchen, NJ: The Scarecrow Press, Inc., 1988.

Pfautsch, Lloyd. *Mental Warmups for the Choral Director*. New York: Lawson-Gould, 1969.

Phillips, Kenneth H. *Basic Techniques of Conducting*. New York: Oxford University Press, 1997.

Rudolf, Max. *The Grammar of Conducting*, 3rd ed. New York: Schirmer Books, 1993.

Telfer, Nancy. *Successful Sight Singing: A Creative, Step by Step Approach*. San Diego, CA: Kjos, 1992. V77T Teacher's Guide; V77S Vocal Edition

Webb, Guy B. *Up Front! Becoming the Complete Choral Conductor*. Boston: ECS, 1993.

Devotional/Theological

Coleman, Gerald Patrick. *How Can I Keep from Singing: Conversations in Renewal for the Church's Musicians*. St. Louis: Concordia, 1991.

Faulkner, Quentin. *Choir Rehearsal Prayers*. St. Louis: MorningStar, 1990.

Orr, N. Lee. *The Church Music Handbook for Pastors and Musicians*. Nashville, TN: Abingdon Press, 1991.

Schalk, Carl. *First Person Singular: Reflections on Worship, Liturgy, and Children*. St. Louis: MorningStar, 1998.

Westermeyer, Paul. Te Deum: *The Church and Music*. Minneapolis: Augsburg Fortress, 1998.

Wold, Wayne L. *Tune My Heart to Sing: Devotions for Choirs*. Minneapolis: Augsburg Fortress, 1997.

Handbells/Instrumental

Folkening, John. *Handbells in the Liturgical Service*. St. Louis: Concordia, 1984.

Behnke, John A. *Successful Ringing: Step by Step*. St. Louis: Concordia, 1999.

Black, Dave, and Tom Gerou. *Essential Dictionary of Orchestration: Ranges, General Characteristics, Technical Considerations, and Scoring Tips*. Los Angeles: Alfred, 1998.

Hendrickson, Clarence V. Handy *Manual Fingering Charts for Instrumentalists*. New York: Carl Fischer, 1957.

Frazier, James, *et al. Handbells in the Liturgy: a Practical Guide for the Use of Handbells in Liturgical Worship*. Sellersville, PA: Schulmerich Carillons, Inc., 1994, published by Concordia.

Voice/Vocal Techniques

Anderson, Richard. *Complete Book of Voice Training*. West Nyack, NY: Parker, 1979.

Burtis, Herbert. *Sing On! Sing On! A Guide to the Life-Long Enjoyment of the Voice for Singers and Teachers of the Vocal Art*. Boston: ECS, 1992.

Cooksey, John M. *Working with Adolescent Voices*. St. Louis: Concordia, 1999.

Ehmann, Wilhelm and Frauke Haasemann. Trans. Brenda Smith. *Voice Building for Choirs*. Chapel Hill, NC: Hinshaw, 1982.

Ammer, Christine. *The A to Z of Foreign Musical Terms*. Boston: ECS, 1988.

Keirsey, David and Marilyn Bates. *Please Understand Me: Character and Temperament Types*, 4th ed. Del Mar, CA: Gnosology Books Ltd., 1984.

Journals

The American Organist (The official journal of the American Guild of Organists) cf. "Easy Service Music," by Marilyn Stulken, a regular feature since December 1998.

Choral Journal (The official journal of the American Choral Directors Association)
Contains numerous articles on every facet of choral directing.

Videotapes

Barresi, Anthony, with John Paul Johnson. *Barresi on Adolescent Voice*. Madison, WI: University of Wisconsin—Madison, 1986.

Boyter, Mabel Stewart. *Guiding the Uncertain Singer*. Garland, TX: Choristers Guild.
(for young singers)

Ehly, Eph. *Choral Singing Style*. Milwaukee: Hal Leonard Publishing Corp., 1988.

Eichenberger, Rodney, with Andre Thomas. *What They See Is What You Get: Linking the visual, the aural, and the kinetic to promote artistic choral singing*. Chapel Hill, NC: Hinshaw, 1994.

Helen Kemp. *A Helen Kemp Portrait*. Garland, TX: Choristers Guild.

Jordan, James. *Evoking Sound: Fundamentals of Choral Conducting and Rehearsing*. Chicago: GIA Publications, 1996.

Marshall, Jane. *Sounds, Scores, and Signals 1*. Garland, TX: Choristers Guild. CGVT1

Marshall, Jane. *Sounds, Scores, and Signals 2*. Garland, TX: Choristers Guild. CGVT 2

Rao, Doreen. *The Children's Choir with Doreen Rao and the Glen Ellyn Children's Chorus*. Lawton, OK: American Choral Directors Association, 1988.

Schultz, Ralph. *Leading the Choir: a Guide for the Inexperienced Choir Director*. St. Louis: Concordia, 1990.

Warland, Dale. *Attention to Detail: a Choral Conductor's Guide*. [U.S.]: American Choral Catalogue, 1994.

Recommended Choral Octavos for SAB Voices

"A Canon of Praise," Natalie Sleeth, kybd, opt hb, Choristers Guild.

"A Shoot Shall Come Forth," Richard Horn, SAB, org, MorningStar.

"A Virgin Most Pure," Kenneth Kosche, SAB, kybd, Concordia.

"Call to Remembrance, O Lord," R. Farrant (arr. Kosche), SAB, opt kybd, Coronet.

"Concordia Classics," David Johnson (ed.), 18 reproducible SAB titles, Concordia.

"Carol of the Gifts," Walter Ehret. SAB, kybd, Theodore Presser.

"Coram Deo, Set I," K. Lee Scott. SAB, kybd, MorningStar.

"Coram Deo, Set II," K. Lee Scott. SAB, kybd, inst, MorningStar.

"Hide Not Thou Thy Face" R. Farrant (arr. Kosche), SAB, opt kybd, Coronet.

"Hymn Stanzas for SAB Choirs, 2," arr. Kenneth Kosche, 12 hymn settings for SAB, kybd, particularly keyed to *LW* and *LBW*, (Baritone has cantus firmus) Concordia.

"If You Will Trust the Lord to Guide You," Kenneth Kosche, SAB, pno, fl, MorningStar.

"In the Manger," John Behnke, SAB, kybd, Concordia.

"I Walk in Danger All the Way," Kenneth Kosche, SAB, opt congr, fl, ob., org, Concordia.

"Like As a Father," Luigi Cherubini (arr. Austin Lovelace), kybd, Choristers Guild.

"Rejoice, Rejoice Believers," K. Lee Scott, SAB, kybd, MorningStar.

"See in Yonder Manger Low," Kenneth Kosche, SAB, kybd, Coronet.

"The SAB Chorale Book," Paul Thomas (ed.), 25 titles SAB, Concordia.

"When All Your Mercies, O My God," Kenneth Kosche, SAB, kybd, Concordia.

CPSIA information can be obtained at www.ICGtesting.com
Printed in the USA
LVOW08s1406051013

355507LV00001B/1/P